MEN OF LIKE PASSION

Dear Jane,

Thank you for <u>all</u> your encouragement to me over the years. God bless your "retiring" years!

Bill Taylor
9-16-11

MEN OF LIKE PASSION

Six Men God Used To Bless His People

BILL TAYLOR

Outskirts Press, Inc.
Denver, Colorado

The opinions expressed in this manuscript are solely the opinions of the author and do not represent the opinions or thoughts of the publisher. The author has represented and warranted full ownership and/or legal right to publish all the materials in this book.

Men of Like Passion
Six Men God Used to Bless His People
All Rights Reserved.
Copyright © 2011 Bill Taylor
v3.0

Cover Photo © 2011 JupiterImages Corporation. All rights reserved - used with permission.

This book may not be reproduced, transmitted, or stored in whole or in part by any means, including graphic, electronic, or mechanical without the express written consent of the publisher except in the case of brief quotations embodied in critical articles and reviews.

Outskirts Press, Inc.
http://www.outskirtspress.com

ISBN: 978-1-4327-7921-4

Outskirts Press and the "OP" logo are trademarks belonging to Outskirts Press, Inc.

PRINTED IN THE UNITED STATES OF AMERICA

Contents

Adam: The First Man 1
   A Creature In God's Image 1
   Man Became A Living Soul 3
   There He Put The Man 5
   The First Law of God 7
   Male and Female: One Unit 9
   Hath God Said? 11
   Where Art Thou? 14
   The Curse of Sin 15
   Knowledge of Good and Evil 18
   A Child is Born 20
   Cain Rose Up 22
   What Hast Thou Done? 24
   Men Called Upon God 25
   A Man Walked With God 27
   And He Died 29

Noah: A Man Who Found Grace 33
   This Shall Be Our Rest 33
   They Corrupted His Way 35
   Come into the Ark 37
   The Rain Upon the Earth 39
   He Sent Forth the Dove 40
   A Sweet Savor 42

The Tents of Shem 44

Abraham: A Man Who Was God's Friend 47
As the Lord Had Spoken 47
There He Built an Altar 49
Down Into Egypt 50
Up Out of Egypt 52
Great Reassurance 54
He Gave Him Tithes of All 55
Counted for Righteousness 57
The Future Declared 59
Too Hard for the Lord? 60
Judge of All the Earth 62
God Remembered Abraham 64
As He Had Spoken 65
The Rule of Fairness 67
Willing to Offer His Son 68
Made Sure for a Possession 70
His Angel Goes Before 72
God Is in the Details 74
Humility in Willingness 75
A Godly Inheritance 78
He Died in Faith 80

Jacob: A Man of Deceit Whom God Loved 83
Two Nations - Two Manner of People 83
The Supplanter 85
The Deceiver 86
Sent Away 88
A Certain Place 90
Behold a Ladder 92
The Lord Is in This Place 94
Jacob Loved Rachel 96
Blessed for Jacob's Sake 97

I Will Be With Thee 99
Her Father's Images 101
Rituals and Emblems 102
God's Host 104
Jacob's Humility 106
A Prince, With God 108
Family Reunion 110
Go Up to Bethel 112
God Almighty Blesses Israel 114
Life Comes from Death 116
Jacob Dwelt In The Land 118
Jacob Rose Up 120
Jacob Blessed Pharaoh 122
Jacob's End 124

Joseph: A Man for Whom God Meant Good 127

Coat of Many Colors 127
Dreamed A Dream 129
The Strength of Grace 130
Sold Into Bondage 132
The Blessing of the Lord 134
Think On Me 138
It Is Not in Me 140
Do What He Says 142
They Bowed Down 144
God Sent Me Here 145
I Will Nourish Thee 148
What Is Your Occupation? 150
Carry Me Out of Egypt 152
They Shall Be Mine 153
A Fruitful Bough 155
God Will Surely Visit You 157

Moses: A Man Chosen to Deliver God's People 161
    The Land Was Filled 161
    They Feared God 163
    A Goodly Child 165
    Drawn Out of the Water 167
    Who Made Thee A Prince? 169
    In Process of Time 171
    Holy Ground 173
    I AM Hath Sent Me 174
    I Will Be With Thy Mouth 177
    Israel Is My Son 178
    The People Believed 180
    Redeemed With Great Judgments 182
    God's Stretched Forth Hand 184
    He Hardened His Heart 186
    Pharaoh's Final Refusal 187
    The Lord's Passover 189
    What Mean Ye by This Service? 190
    Not by the Easy Way 192
    To Go by Day and Night 193
    Overtaken by the Sea 195
    Stand Still, Then Go Forward 197
    Walked Upon Dry Land 198
    The Song of Moses 200

Adam: The First Man

A Creature In God's Image

"And God said, Let us make man in our image, after our likeness: and let them have dominion over the fish of the sea, and over the fowl of the air, and over the cattle, and over all the earth, and over every creeping thing that creepeth upon the earth. So God created man in his own image, in the image of God created he him; male and female created he them." Genesis 1:26-27

On the sixth day of Creation, God completed His work in a final act of grace and glory. He had created the heavens and the earth, populating them with heavenly bodies and earthly living things. The sun, moon, and stars shone in all their illuminating glory, and the earth was fully capable of thriving and continuing on the path its Creator had established for it. He had spoken all things into existence by the power of His word, simply stating, "Let there be..." and that which He commanded came together in perfect alignment with His purpose and will. He commanded, "Let the earth bring forth..." and it responded perfectly and exactly to His powerful word. Yet, in the final act of His glorious Creation, God did not issue commandments to the elements that would form man. He did not speak man into existence as He had every other animate and inanimate part of His Creation; rather, God spoke with Himself: "Let us make man." The evidence of perfect agreement between the Triune Godhead is abundant in Creation. The Genesis account tells us first, "In the beginning God created." From that we can be assured of the Father's Presence. We can also be assured that the Holy Spirit of God was there, because He "moved upon the face of the deep," that God had spoken into existence out of nothing. We can also be assured of the Presence of Christ, the eternal Son of God, at Creation. The Apostle John tells us in his Gospel, "In the beginning was the word, and the word was with God, and the word was God." Here, the three-in-one God worked in perfect agreement with the counsel of His own will in Creating the heavens and the earth; but the clearest evidence of His perfect will is found in man's creation.

When God took counsel with Himself and said, "Let us make man," He was not merely adding another living being to His long list of creatures. This last element of Creation was different. He bore the image of His Creator. Now we might rightfully argue that all Creation bears the mark of its Creator, but man did not just bear the mark of God; he was formed to bear the very image of God. "Let us make man in our image, after our likeness," God counseled with Himself. Before we venture off into speculation that we can know what God looks like physically, let's try to understand what this really means. Man's physical image is a refection - and merely one reflection - of God's nature. He made man upright. No matter what the evolutionist may want to believe about man crawling around on all fours, he was created to stand erect and walk on two legs. This reflects his God-given position in Creation of dominion over every other living thing. We know this is true, because God brought the other living things to the man for him to give them names. Let's set the physical image aside, however, to fully understand man in God's image. God's great love and careful attention was evident in this last act of Creation, "And the LORD God formed man of the dust of the ground, and breathed into his nostrils the breath of life; and man became a living soul" (Genesis 2:7). He formed man's physical being using the lowliest elements of the earth - the dust. Glory in that if you can. It is what God did to give man life that reflects His image. He "breathed into his nostrils the breath of life; and man became a living soul." Only man - the final part of God's Creation - was given a soul. And it was a "living" soul as first given to Adam. By this one act, God opened the way for a lowly creature formed from the dust of the earth to know its Creator, and to have communion with Him! We shall explore the wondrous glory - and the limits - of this precious truth in days to come.

It is good to praise the wondrous works of our Creator God.

Man Became A Living Soul

"And the LORD God formed man of the dust of the ground, and breathed into his nostrils the breath of life; and man became a living soul." Genesis 2:7

God created the heavens and the earth, and He created all living things in them by the word of His commandment. The animate objects of His Creation lived and moved according to the directing power of His word. Every creature of this type that breathes, lives, and moves does so because God commanded it to be so. Their animation was part and parcel to the act of their creation, and they still act instinctively according to the Creation laws of God. Trees and other plants have life, but they do not move other than by the force of the wind God created. Animals have life, and they move; so they are a step above plant life in their ability to have some control over their fate. Still, the animals operate according to the pattern their Creator established for them. They act by instinct, which He gave them to use as they live their lives on the earth. Animals appear to exhibit emotions, such as love and anger; but they only appear to do so because humans look at their instinctive behavior and believe it to be similar to human behavior. Animals do not think or reason, they operate by God-given instinct. Even newborn animals quickly exhibit many of the characteristics and traits that their parents have. It is born in them. They can learn, but they learn by instinct. This is not so with man. He alone operates with the capability to plan, reason, analyze, and think. His emotions are the result of his unique standing as the ultimate of God's Creation.

After God created the man from the dust of earth, by determined action rather than by speaking, He "breathed into his nostrils the breath of life." A seventeenth century Bible scholar, John Gill, said this of God's breathing into man the breath of life: "...which in that way entered into his body, and quickened it, which before was a lifeless lump of clay, though beautifully shapen: it is in the plural number, the "breath of lives" (l), including the vegetative, sensitive, and rational life of man. And this was produced not with his body, as the souls of brutes were, and was produced by the breath of God, as theirs were not; nor theirs out of the earth, as his body was: and these two different productions show the different nature of the soul and body of man, the one is material and mortal, the other immaterial and immortal:" Understanding the difference between man and animals, and between his body and his soul, is crucial to understanding how deep God's love for His people goes. He created man to think, to rationalize, to be able to commune with Him on a basis of will and knowledge, and not on the basis of instinct. This communion was not to gain eternal standing with God - He had made supreme provision for that - it was so that man could rejoice in the spiritual blessings of his relationship with God. Even after the man He created rebelled, disobeyed the loving command of His Creator, and plunged all of his progeny into a state of sin and death by sin, God continued to draw His people to experience communion with Him. He did so through the agency of their own ability to reason (recognize sin in their lives) and react according to good reasoning (repent and return to Him). The prophet Isaiah tells us that God spoke to Israel in their open rebellion to tell them that He had provided the only remedy for their sins. "Come now, and let us reason together, saith the LORD: though your sins be as scarlet, they shall be as white as snow; though they be red like crimson, they shall be as wool. If ye be willing and obedient, ye shall eat the good of the land: But if ye refuse and rebel, ye shall be devoured with the sword: for the mouth of the LORD hath spoken it" Isaiah 1:18-20. This two-part reassurance would do an unthinking, unfeeling animal no good; but much good could come to the man whose soul did God give and who had been made spiritually alive by His in-breathing. God's assurance to them was that they were His eternally by His own provision, and that they could enjoy the blessings of that relationship in time by their obedience. Their disobedience would not negate the eternal aspects of God's love, but it would separate them from enjoying the "good of the (spiritual) land." God made man in His image, and man would fall from that image through his disobedience; but God would send a perfect man to restore that image. Yes, man is the ultimate of God's Creation. He is the beginning and He is the end.

It is good to thank God for His eternal provision of salvation and His deliverance to communion with Him in time.

There He Put The Man

"And the LORD God planted a garden eastward in Eden; and there he put the man whom he had formed. And out of the ground made the LORD God to grow every tree that is pleasant to the sight, and good for food; the tree of life also in the midst of the garden, and the tree of knowledge of good and evil." Genesis 2:8-9

"And the LORD God took the man, and put him into the garden of Eden to dress it and to keep it." Genesis 2:15

There are still some people today who want to argue whether or not God has the right to do with His Creation whatever He pleases. Many of these same people believe that God created the heavens and the earth and then simply stepped back and let them go - to end up wherever they happened to end up. For the inanimate elements of Creation, such as the planets on the larger scale and the earthly elements on the smaller scale, God set them in their prescribed courses and they operate according to His "motivation," so to speak. The plants and animal life on earth still operate according to the pattern and method their Creator assigned them. In this aspect, God never relinquished control of His Creation. He still is in control of it today. It is when we consider man, and the characteristic many believe controls him most strongly - his free will - that it causes those who question God's participation to come to a theological, or philosophical, place referred to as "deism," which is the belief that God created, then let His Creation operate by itself. The very first action God took concerning the man whom He had just created ought to show us that deism will not hold up to honest inspection as a valid view of God and His nature. The evidence is that God created - and fully furnished - the place where He intended man to live; and then He put the man where He wanted him to be.

First, God planted a garden eastward in Eden. This is so rich in spiritual meaning! God, Who spoke all things into existence and Who graciously and purposely formed man from the dust of the earth, is shown by these words to provide and arrange a place of great beauty and substance so that the man would have a special place in which to dwell. The fact that He planted the garden shows His loving provision of all good things, and that He planted it eastward - or toward the east - follows the pattern of His assurance of redemption coming from the east. There God made the source of man's subsistence - every tree that is pleasant to the sight, and good for food. He also placed the tree of life, the symbol of God's provision of salvation, in the midst of the garden; and the tree of the knowledge of good and evil was there as well. God prepared the place where man could eat and live while he enjoyed the very sight of all that God had provided for him. This doesn't seem much like deism, does it? It seems more like the true picture of our loving, providing God, Who has acted with will and purpose toward His people. God did not leave it up to the man to find his way to the garden He had created specifically for the man. God put the man there, by directed and purposeful action. It was His will to do so, and He did what He purposed to do. Did he violate the man's will by doing so? Was the man merely a puppet? No, God allowed the man to operate freely - within the bounds of His provision and His direction. We shall see in coming days how that God gave man free access to all He had provided for him, with one stated exception. There was one guiding principle, one commandment, and it contained blessings for obedience and consequences for disobedience. The man was free to enjoy the great provision of good things his Creator made for him. Not only so, but God also gave man a work to do. This was not to till the ground and make things grow as some assume. That would come later, after he disobeyed God's command. The work he had to do was to "dress and keep" the garden. That meant to hold God's provision in reverence and to continue to observe the goodness it imparted to his existence. A later commandment would follow this pattern when God said that His people were to, "remember the Sabbath day to keep it holy." Surely this provides ample proof that God did not "step back," but, rather, He actively led the man to enjoy the goodness of communion with his Creator. This pattern still holds true today concerning the salvation of God's people: God planted a place of spiritual subsistence, and He actively places His people there to freely operate within the bounds of His provision.

It is good to observe the place where God has put us, then dress it and keep it.

The First Law of God

"And the LORD God commanded the man, saying, Of every tree of the garden thou mayest freely eat: But of the tree of the knowledge of good and evil, thou shalt not eat of it: for in the day that thou eatest thereof thou shalt surely die." Genesis 2:16-17

◄ MEN OF LIKE PASSION

The Creator of all things had all power and authority to specify exactly the terms and conditions under which His Creation would operate. The heavens and the earth were set in operation by certain natural laws and they still operate accordingly. One example is the law of gravity on the earth. That law serves to allow living beings and non-living objects unattached to the earth to remain on the earth. The laws of nature ensure that plant and animal life follows a certain cycle by which these objects of God's Creation live and reproduce themselves. All of nature operates according to these laws, which require no understanding, reasoning, or knowledge of the consequences for disobedience on the part of their subjects; but God gave another law that did not apply to plants and animals, a law based on a moral code. When we talk about morals, we can only apply that to mankind. There are certainly no moral requirements for non-living elements of God's Creation. Living plants and animals do not have morals, nor do they require them. Morals have to do with creatures that have the ability to hear, understand, and rationalize. God's first law outside of the natural laws inherent in His Creating authority was a moral law given to the man He created and put in the garden that He had prepared for him to enjoy and be sustained by.

The basis of all moral laws is liberty. A moral law assumes the ability of its subjects to keep it, but it also assumes the possibility of its subjects to break it, and assigns liability on that basis. Here is the authority of God's first law: "...the LORD God commanded the man." He spoke directly to the man, telling Him what He could do and what he could not do. Along with that authority and direction was the prescribed penalty for the breaking of God's law. Nothing could have been clearer. Today we have lawyers who spend their lives trying to achieve an interpretation of laws that will give their clients the advantage. They look for the "gray areas" of understanding and try to show precedent where the law is not clear and could be interpreted to suit their case. God's first law had no gray areas, nor was there any precedent. The man He created stood before Him, heard His commandment, and fully understood both its privileges brought by obedience and its consequences brought by disobedience. He understood, he reasoned, he knew. God created him to be able to do so. We think of laws as being restrictive, but with liberty as their foundation they are not at all restrictive to anyone except those who are prone to break them. God's law established moral boundaries. The man was able to freely walk within the boundaries of God's first moral law. We tend to think of what the law forbids, but listen to what it allowed as its first point: "Of every tree of the garden thou mayest freely eat." Nothing that was good for him was forbidden to the man - only that which was bad for him was forbidden. There was only one tree specified of which he was not to eat - the tree of the knowledge of good and evil. God not only prescribed the law of liberty in that first commandment, but He also prescribed the law of death. He spoke judgment against sin when He prescribed the penalty for disobedience to His law, saying, "For in the day that thou eatest thereof thou shalt surely die." The man understood, and we shall see what terrible effects his actions concerning God's law had on every future living person.

It is good to consider the wondrous liberty of God's law, and walk in that knowledge.

Male and Female: One Unit

"And the LORD God caused a deep sleep to fall upon Adam, and he slept: and he took one of his ribs, and closed up the flesh instead thereof; And the rib, which the LORD God had taken from man, made he a woman, and brought her unto the man. And Adam said, This is now bone of my bones, and flesh of my flesh: she shall be called Woman, because she was taken out of Man. Therefore shall a man leave his father and his mother, and shall cleave unto his wife: and they shall be one flesh. And they were both naked, the man and his wife, and were not ashamed." Genesis 2:21-25

MEN OF LIKE PASSION

The timing and the order in which God created the father and mother of all mankind is often treated with much analysis and speculation. Many are not willing to take the clear wording of Scripture, inferring from it that God somehow made the woman inferior to the man. This is not true, and is not what God's word tells us. Genesis 1:27-28 says, "So God created man in his own image, in the image of God created he him; male and female created he them. And God blessed them, and God said unto them, Be fruitful, and multiply, and replenish the earth, and subdue it: and have dominion over the fish of the sea, and over the fowl of the air, and over every living thing that moveth upon the earth." In this passage we see the essence of the relationship of the man to the woman, and of both of them to God. He created man (mankind) in His own image, male and female. Now the purpose of this is not to play into the modern method of trying to make man and woman equal in all things, so that social consciousness and opinion will be appeased; instead, we need to understand this so we may clearly understand God's imprinting Himself on mankind. He did not do so to make the man greater than the woman; neither did He do so to make the woman more important than the man. God recorded this in His word so that we may see that the basis of His dealing with mankind was going to be the family - man and woman becoming one flesh - because He made the first pair of one flesh. Adam acknowledged God's dominion in this part of Creation when he took on headship of and responsibility for the woman, "This is now bone of my bones, and flesh of my flesh: she shall be called Woman, because she was taken out of Man." She was bone of his bones, flesh of his flesh; and Adam spoke these words in recognition that they were made one unit.

Next, Adam spoke of which he knew nothing by practical experience: "Therefore shall a man leave his father and his mother, and shall cleave unto his wife: and they shall be one flesh." These words were for all future generations. The institute of marriage, and that of one man to one woman exclusively, was established through Adam's words, but by God's direction. This left no room for polygamy, and no room for same sex "marriages" (so-called). The only way these have ever existed is in the imaginations of people who will not accept the clear direction of God's word. The marriage between Adam and Eve (as he would name her) formed the basis for every human being that has been born since that time. Every society that has existed from that time has recognized marriage, even if some have tried to alter its form. Adam and Eve were husband and wife, and God Himself performed the "ceremony". The state in which marriage was instituted was a pure, sinless state. This is typified by the innocent state in which Adam and Eve were joined together, "And they were both naked, the man and his wife, and were not ashamed." Perverted minds have been trying for thousands of years to allow people to walk around naked, but there is an underlying shame attached to that state now. That shame was not a part of God's Creation: mankind brought it about; but when Adam and Eve were joined together, they knew no shame. They did not know they were naked. Look at this statement, and imagine how you would feel if you were out in public without any clothes on. You know very well that you would try to hide your nakedness if you were in your right mind. That is our state since Adam and Eve fell from their innocent state; but in its inception, marriage was shown to be a pure state by their nakedness. Yes, God instituted marriage - between one man and one woman - and He has not changed the concept of family as the basis of His dealing with mankind.

It is good to thank God that our society has always been based upon the concept of marriage: male and female - one unit.

Hath God Said?

"Now the serpent was more subtle than any beast of the field which the LORD God had made. And he said unto the woman, Yea, hath God said, Ye shall not eat of every tree of the garden? And the woman said unto the serpent, We may eat of the fruit of the trees of the garden: But of the fruit of the tree which is in the midst of the garden, God hath said, Ye shall not eat of it, neither shall ye touch it, lest ye die. And the serpent said unto the woman, Ye shall not surely die" Genesis 3:1-4.

God made a perfect place for mankind to inhabit, placed him there, and gave him complete liberty to eat of every tree in the garden, except one. He issued a commandment concerning that tree: "But of the tree of the knowledge of good and evil, thou shalt not eat of it: for in the day that thou eatest thereof thou shalt surely die" (Genesis 2:17). There does not seem to be much about what God said or the way He said it that could leave room for interpretation does there? God did not go to great lengths to explain all the reasons He said for the man not to eat of this tree. It was enough that He said, "Ye shall not eat of it, neither shall ye touch it." Complete avoidance was the only way that mankind could satisfy God's righteous demands. Adam knew this. God spoke the commandment to him. He obviously conveyed this to Eve, his wife; but obviously she was subject to being deceived about God's intent when He issued the commandment. Anytime there is a possibility of our being deceived or confused about something God has said, there appears the greatest of all Deceivers - Satan. Our first view of this "accuser of the brethren" was when he confronted Eve with her confusion. He was typified in the Genesis account as a serpent and it was said of him that he, "was more subtle than any beast of the field which the LORD God had made." Was this really a talking snake? Is this the reason the majority of mankind still fears snakes today? These are questions that can get us off the main subject, just as Satan got Eve off the main subject by asking her what she thought God had said.

Interpretation of God's commandments has been the undoing of many since Eve entered into a philosophical discussion with Satan. When we look for shades of gray, or areas where what God has said on any subject seems open to our own interpretation, we're right where Eve

ADAM: THE FIRST MAN

stood. The Hebrew word for "serpent" can mean "hiss," or "sting." Let's use the latter for just a moment. God's word tells us that sin is the "sting" of death. Sin is also the transgression of God's law. As Eve stood reasoning with the serpent, she made herself subject to the sting of death. Satan knew exactly what God had said. He was not seeking further understanding. His objective was then what it is now. Peter used another animal to describe Satan: "your adversary the devil, as a roaring lion, walketh about, seeking whom he may devour:" (I Peter 5:8). His devouring is not of an eternal nature, where this concerns God's children. He is not able to do that. What he can do, however, is cause God's people to question God, to look for "gray areas" in what He has commanded. Why does Satan do this? He does so to try to steal God's power and glory and assume it for himself. We pretty well understand that. The real question is why do we do this? Why did Eve stand discussing this with the serpent when all she had to do was trust and obey her gracious Creator? Yes, the old Deceiver Satan is subtle; and yes, Eve was deceived; but all she had to do was accept what God said without question. In the military, blind obedience to commands must be tempered with at least one question: "Is this a lawful order? Have I just been issued an order that will break some law?" If it is a lawful order, a military man must obey without questioning. If it is not, he is free to disobey. Satan was really asking Eve, "Did God have the right to withhold the tree of the knowledge of good and evil from you? Is He really able to stop you from eating of its fruit? Or, does He know that your eating of that fruit will give you real liberty and power equal to His?" Sin always promises liberty but can only deliver bondage. Satan's great lie, "Ye shall not surely die," delivered the shades of gray. No, they would not immediately die a physical death, but death awaited Adam and Eve when they ate of the fruit that God had commanded them not to eat. Whether deceived, as Eve, or not deceived, as Adam, the end result of sin is always death. James said, "But every man is tempted, when he is drawn away of his own lust, and enticed. Then when lust hath conceived, it bringeth forth sin: and sin, when it is finished, bringeth forth death" (James 1:14-15).

MEN OF LIKE PASSION

It is good to remember that God's word tells us to resist the Devil and he will flee from us.

Where Art Thou?

"And the LORD God called unto Adam, and said unto him, Where art thou?" Genesis 3:9

Deceived by the subtlety of that old serpent, the Devil, Eve "took of the fruit thereof, and did eat, and gave also unto her husband with her; and he did eat." The serpent had planted a seed of doubt in her mind by making the one thing that God had withheld from mankind seem very alluring to her. Satan told Eve that God was not allowing her and Adam to eat of that one thing because it would open their eyes and make them "as gods, knowing good and evil." The seed of doubt soon sprouted into a plant ready to bear the fruit of sin and rebellion when Eve, "saw that the tree was good for food, and that it was pleasant to the eyes, and a tree to be desired to make one wise." Here are the three conditions of potential sin that the Apostle John would later name: the lust of the eyes, the lust of the flesh, and the pride of life. Wait a minute! God told them they could eat of every tree that was good for them in the Garden, but she now saw that this one was also good for food. Why would God withhold something that looked so good? Once she saw this, Eve began to see how pleasant the forbidden fruit was to look at, and finally she saw that eating this fruit could also "make one wise." I remember hearing people some four decades ago speaking of how they wanted to experience everything in life they could experience, so they could be well rounded. God is very familiar with this line of reasoning - it started in mankind with Eve. The Bible book of Ecclesiastes was written to chronicle the effects of giving oneself to the pursuit of this same fruit. Solomon determined he would not withhold any experience from his senses, but in the end all he could say was, "all is vanity." Eve and her husband Adam were about to experience the emptiness that pursuing forbidden fruit brings to God's people.

ADAM: THE FIRST MAN

Eve ate first of the fruit God had forbidden; then she gave it to Adam, and "he did eat." She was deceived, but he ate knowingly. He knew the results. Why did he choose to openly disobey God? Men have speculated about this since that day, but why Adam disobeyed God matters less than the fact that he did so. He was immediately charged with the crime, and he knew that he was guilty. God had already set the penalty. Judgment was set, and death was the result. Corruption immediately set in. Before they sinned, Adam and Eve did not know they were naked; now, they immediately knew their state and feared to be seen this way. Satan did not tell them they were naked, and God certainly did not do so; the full effects of judgment for disobedience of God's law "told" them they were naked. They knew good and evil. They had only known good before they sinned; but now they knew there were two states of existence and they could see the awful effects of the latter. Adam and Eve tried to cover their own sins, typified by sewing fig leaves together to cover their nakedness. Their poor attempt was futile. Man cannot cover - atone for - his own sins! Realizing this, they hid themselves from God. Impossible! When God called out, "Where art thou?" it was not so He could find this out. He knew exactly where they were. He asked the question so they could see "where" they were: sinners, trying to hide their sin from God. The wonderful part of this sad story is that God did not leave them in their sad state. They would pay the penalty prescribed by law, but God would graciously clothe them and hide their sins.

It is good to thank God for the clothing of His righteousness to cover our sins.

The Curse of Sin

"And the LORD God said unto the serpent, Because thou hast done this, thou art cursed above all cattle, and above every beast of the field; upon thy belly shalt thou go, and dust shalt thou eat all the days of thy life: And I will put enmity between thee and the woman, and between thy seed and her seed; it shall bruise thy head, and thou shalt bruise his heel." Genesis 3:14-15

Having eaten of the forbidden fruit, Adam immediately began to show the effects of sin now working in him. The Lord asked Adam a direct question that would have given him the opportunity to openly confess his sin, "Hast thou eaten of the tree, whereof I commanded thee that thou shouldest not eat?" His response showed his and every future man's natural response to God's declaration of sin: he tried to pass the guilt of disobedience off of his shoulders onto someone else's. It was not his fault, by Adam's reasoning. The woman, he said, it was the woman. She gave me to eat, and I ate. This was as if to say, "It really wasn't my fault." In fact, Adam went so far as to blame God, saying, "The woman whom thou gavest to be with me, she gave me of the tree, and I did eat." This first attempt to pass the blame then went to the next step. Eve blamed the serpent, saying he, "beguiled me, and I did eat." They each were going to bear the blame for their own actions, even though God held Adam ultimately responsible, as head of the family. Adam was not only guilty because of his position as head, but he also was "not deceived." He knew what God had said, and he knew the judgment God had pronounced for disobedience. The woman was "beguiled," or deceived by the serpent's twisting of what God had said and questioning His real meaning. Each of them, the man, the woman, and the serpent received a pronouncement of the penalty associated with their continued existence on earth as they awaited the ultimate carrying out of God's judgment: "In the day that thou eatest thereof thou shalt surely die."

Death was the sentence to be carried out, and there was more than one application of death - separation - that was about to take place. The man and woman would be expelled from the Garden of Eden, never to see it again. Never again would they have open and free communion with their Creator in the freedom of innocence. Their existence had once been one of liberty and joy as they enjoyed all that

ADAM: THE FIRST MAN

the Garden provided them at God's command, but from that point on things would be hard for them - until they died. The attempt to pass blame had gone from the man to the woman to the serpent; now God began pronouncing the penalties associated with their actions first to the serpent, then to the woman, and finally to the man. God cursed the serpent and sentenced him to an earthly existence of eating dust as he crawled around on his belly, lower than every other creature. The ultimate "curse" God pronounced on the serpent was actually a final judgment pronounced on Satan, when God foretold of the One He would send to overcome the power and curse of sin and satisfy God's righteous judgment, "And I will put enmity between thee and the woman, and between thy seed and her seed; it shall bruise thy head, and thou shalt bruise his heel." This foretold of the Lord, Jesus Christ, Whose death on the Cross would "bruise" the head of Satan. The woman was going to experience sorrow in childbirth and subjection to the authority of the man. Eve had been on equal footing with Adam in the Garden prior to her launching out on her own in dealing with the serpent, but her disobedience would subject her to his "rule" over her all the days of her life. The state of the man was to be opposite to what he had enjoyed in the Garden. There, God had provided all he needed, causing the good things to grow and replenish themselves for Adam's enjoyment. Outside the Garden, and due to his disobedience, Adam would have to till the ground to raise his own food, constantly fight against the thorns and thistles that tried to choke out Adam's work, and labor by the sweat of his brow until he returned to the dust from which God formed him. Paul would later say, "...the wages of sin is death." God cursed Satan's existence, cursed Eve's earthly role to one of child bearing and subjection, and cursed the ground for Adam's sake. The curse of sin had earthly consequences in their continued experience, and the end of their earthly existence would be brought about by the ultimate curse of death by sin. Many people spend a lot of time trying to determine the cause of death in its victims: sin is the cause of death. Both the guilty and the "innocent" victims pay the price of the curse of sin that resulted from

Adam's disobedience; but the "Seed of the woman" (Christ) was the only one who could pay the ultimate price God demanded.

It is good to rejoice in the fact that God provided the remedy for the curse of sin - the Sinless Blood of His Son, Jesus Christ.

Knowledge of Good and Evil

"And the LORD God said, Behold, the man is become as one of us, to know good and evil: and now, lest he put forth his hand, and take also of the tree of life, and eat, and live forever: Therefore the LORD God sent him forth from the garden of Eden, to till the ground from whence he was taken. So he drove out the man; and he placed at the east of the garden of Eden Cherubims, and a flaming sword which turned every way, to keep the way of the tree of life." Genesis 3:22-24

Did Satan Speak the truth to Eve when he tempted her to eat of that which God forbade? He told her that the only reason God would not allow the woman and her husband to eat the fruit of the tree of the knowledge of good and evil was that, having done so, they would "be as gods, knowing good and evil." Isn't that the very thing God now affirms? Yes, but there is one sad fact about this: the only thing that eating of the forbidden fruit could add to Adam and Eve was to know evil. Before this, they knew good - only good. Hence, the concept of Paradise is to know only good. Everything was good. There are little sayings today where people proclaim things like, "I'm good," when asked if they need anything - meaning that they have no needs. Others will say of certain situations, "It's all good." The only reason anyone will say it's all good is because they are calling some things good that are clearly evil. It was different with Adam and Eve before they disobeyed God. Their existence truly was all good. In fact, they had the power of God's own proclamation to attest to that being the condition of Paradise. After He had created all things in six days, He "saw that it was good," and rested from

ADAM: THE FIRST MAN

His labors on the seventh day of Creation. After Adam's sin, it was no longer all good. The reason was that now God's righteous anger against sin would underlie all things until the fulfillment of His sovereign decree of grace, typified by the Seed of the woman (Christ) bruising the head of the serpent (sin). Adam and Eve did not just know the difference between good and evil, they actually knew - experienced - both these conditions.

In that knowledge they possessed in part the knowledge God had of both good and evil. Their knowledge was not perfect and without impurity, as was God's. He knew evil not because He experienced it, but because He is fully sovereign and all knowing. How could God judge evil and sin if He did not know all about them. Now, it is rightly said that God cannot look upon sin with the least of allowances; but this implies that He will not abide sin, He will not allow it to stand unjudged for what it is - an offense to His holy character. Man is just the opposite. He will abide sin, and he will allow evil to stand unjudged as long as it apparently does him no harm. Adam knew evil now as he had before only known good, and God knew that in man's fallen state his tendency would be to choose evil over good. Why then did He say, "and now, lest he put forth his hand, and take also of the tree of life, and eat, and live forever"? There have been countless speculative discussions about what this means; but the most fitting meaning to its Scriptural context seems to be that man, of his own strength and from his own understanding, cannot "eat" of the symbol of Christ's Presence among God's people - and he certainly cannot do so in his sinful state. God was going to provide the means by which His people would enjoy the fruits of eternal life as they walk here, and the means of doing so can only come because sin was crucified in Christ's flesh. The new creature formed in us by the Holy Spirit of God did not come by inheritance from Adam; instead, we are once again able to know good, and have fellowship with God, because of the righteousness of Jesus Christ imputed to us in the New Birth. Adam's only hope of this was to be "concluded under sin," as Paul stated it in the Roman

Epistle, expelled from the Garden, which he knew only by nature, so that he might be given the hope of Christ.

It is good to rejoice that God "hath begotten us again unto a lively hope." That hope is not to for us to be reinstated into a natural Garden of Paradise, but it is the hope of Christ.

A Child is Born

"And Adam knew Eve his wife; and she conceived, and bore Cain, and said, I have gotten a man from the LORD. And she again bore his brother Abel. And Abel was a keeper of sheep, but Cain was a tiller of the ground." Genesis 4:1-2

Adam was given the command to "be fruitful and multiply," before he ever sinned and was dispelled from God's beautiful Garden of Eden. It would be mere speculation to think of the way or the results of his having followed God's command in his sinless state; furthermore, it is fruitless to speculate upon such, because we are told of his obedience to that command after he fell from his previous sinless state. As Adam and Eve began their new life outside the Garden, a life of toil and trouble, they followed nature as husband and wife. The Bible's statement, "And Adam knew Eve his wife," shows that the child born as a result of that "knowledge" was born as every child has been since: as a result of the union of a man and woman. Eve conceived, and bore Cain. There is absolutely no doubt that at that point she knew the full effect of God's pronouncement of the effects of sin, "Unto the woman he said, I will greatly multiply thy sorrow and thy conception; in sorrow thou shalt bring forth children;" This foretelling of sorrow may have predicted an emotional expression, but is also was showing the physical agony and pain a woman experiences in childbirth. The circumstances of bearing children under the curse of Adamic sin are shown throughout God's word. David said, " Behold, I was shapen in iniquity; and in sin did my mother conceive me" (Psalm 51:5). Job

ADAM: THE FIRST MAN

said, "Man that is born of a woman is of few days, and full of trouble" (Job 14:1). Like most women, Eve did not see or feel the trouble that would eventually come as a result of her having born Cain. She considered his birth a blessing from God; in fact, she thought Cain's birth was the end of their troubles.

"I have gotten a man from the LORD," she proclaimed. Was she just praising God for her son, or was there more to it in her mind? After all, God had promised redemption from sin through the Seed of the woman; and it appears that she thought this was the fulfillment of that promise. There are at least two things that we can glean from this: first, Eve desired an end to the condition that resulted from Adamic sin. She did not love the conditions that resulted from the effects of that sin. Her husband toiled by the sweat of his brow to bring forth food from tilling the ground. Thorns and thistles abounded to try to choke out the very means of their existence. It was a hard life. The second thing about Eve's belief surrounding the birth of her son was the most meaningful, however, from a spiritual standpoint. Eve had a hope of the Redeemer, and not just a natural hope, filled with desire to better their physical circumstances. Her hope was built on the promise of that One Who would "bruise the serpent's head." In a spiritual sense, she must have been "hungry, and faint, and poor," as the old song states the condition of one desiring to see the Savior. She was anticipating His glorious appearing. She did not understand that His being the "Seed" of the woman would mean he could not have Adam as his father, neither any other man with Adam's blood coursing through his veins. That first man, born of the woman, was conceived in sin. The Promised One could not, would not, come this way. Still, Eve had hope, "And she again bore his brother Abel." The evidence of sin's full effect would be realized in these first two men, but God's people continued to look for the Promised One, in every birth of a son. The prophet Isaiah would clarify the condition of His appearing - born of a virgin, God with us. The fullness of the hope was then revealed, "For unto us a child is born, unto us a son is given:

and the government shall be upon his shoulder: and his name shall be called Wonderful, Counselor, The mighty God, The everlasting Father, The Prince of Peace" (Isaiah 9:6).

It is good to remember, "unto us a Son is given."

Cain Rose Up

"And Cain talked with Abel his brother: and it came to pass, when they were in the field, that Cain rose up against Abel his brother, and slew him. And the LORD said unto Cain, Where is Abel thy brother? And he said, I know not: Am I my brother's keeper?" Genesis 4:8-9

The full effect of Adamic sin did not take long to develop after Eve bore Cain, and then a second son Abel. One of the first manifestations of that sin was jealousy. Fully grown, the two brothers pursued their lives and livelihood. Cain was a tiller of the ground and Abel was a keeper of sheep. Their respective positions showed that Cain's means of a living represented the "curse" God pronounced upon Adam for his disobedience, that he would make a hard living by tilling the earth by the sweat of his brow. Abel's means of living, however, was more attuned to the remedy for sin that God had provided while Adam and Eve were still in the Garden. The Lord clothed them with the sin of an animal - probably a sheep - and Abel was a keeper of sheep. That was not the only difference between Cain and Abel, but it was likely the first seed of jealousy in Cain that would later bear tragic fruit. An interesting fact is that they offered sacrifices to the Lord, showing that there was still the knowledge of God in the Adamic family and a desire to establish communion with Him. We see that first in Cain, who "brought of the fruit of the ground an offering unto the LORD." We are then told, " Abel, he also brought of the firstlings of his flock and of the fat thereof." It appears that both men sought God and desired to please Him, but appearances can be misleading.

ADAM: THE FIRST MAN

The next step in the development of jealousy between the brethren was that God was pleased with Abel's sacrifice, but not with Cain's. Now, there is much speculation on why this was so; but the real reason appears to be more with the intent of the offering than with the type. Under the Mosaic Law, an offering of meal - such as Cain's - was perfectly acceptable with God. True, certain offerings specified the requirement for an animal to be slain, and that is what Abel brought; but the real reason God had respect to Abel's offering and not Cain's was the intent of their respective hearts. We are told in God's word that, "without faith it is impossible" to please God. In that same passage, however, we are assured that "He is a rewarder of them that earnestly seek Him." The real difference between Abel and Cain was that Abel earnestly sought God, and sought to please Him. His sacrifice was from the heart, "...of the firstlings of his flock and of the fat thereof." We are told of Cain's offering simply that he brought an offering of the fruit of the ground. God had respect to Abel's offering because by it he sought to honor and worship God. Cain apparently did not have the same desire, bringing an offering out of perceived necessity, and "duty became a load and worship seemed a task" to him. At any rate, God did not accept his offering, and Cain became so angry and jealous of his brother that he slew him. The first murder on earth was because of jealousy. Have you ever been jealous of someone else? Has that ever taken place because they received more attention in things concerning the church than you received? If so, the same Adamic sin - or at least that part of it - was shown to be in full operation still today. God gave the remedy to Cain before he slew his brother: God will accept the offering of those who "do well." This can only be done through the righteousness of Jesus Christ, the only Remedy for Adamic sin. Cain did not desire to please God, because he did not believe that "He is, and that He is a rewarder of them that diligently seek Him." His desire was toward sin, and he pursued that desire by enticing his brother into the field, where he "rose up against Abel his brother, and slew him."

◄ MEN OF LIKE PASSION

It is good to diligently seek God and thank Him for His gracious sin Remedy - without whom we would be as Cain was.

What Hast Thou Done?

"And the LORD said unto Cain, Where is Abel thy brother? And he said, I know not: Am I my brother's keeper? And he said, What hast thou done? the voice of thy brother's blood crieth unto me from the ground." Genesis 4:9-10

Just as He did with Adam's sin in the Garden, God immediately knew and dealt with Cain's sin. The questions He asked Cain were not to aggravate him or entrap him - the Lord knew the answers already. Instead they were as questions asked in a court of law, to establish the facts and have the person being examined state what has happened with his own mouth, thereby establishing the righteousness of whatever judgment is laid down. God's first question, "Where is Abel thy brother?" brought Cain's first attempt to cover one sin with another. "I know not," he lied. Then, going further in his sin and disobedience, he challenged God with, "Am I my brother's keeper?" This question has echoed throughout time since that day, along with various shades of answers to it, usually coming from those like Cain who wish to deflect some measure of guilt from themselves to another. Cain was indeed his brother's keeper, in terms of human compassion and interaction. God's rule over humanity, brought about by His being our Creator, was established with certain "natural" laws. These natural laws would be spoken as spiritual laws through Moses many years later, one of which was, "Thou shalt not kill." However, the absence of spoken law, where God's imprint on humanity is concerned, is no excuse; He created man to be a thinking, rational being, not driven by animalistic emotions. Even man's totally depraved nature, brought about by Adam's sin and imparting the tendency to commit such a foul act as murder, did not give him the freedom to act from that depraved nature. God's question, "What hast thou done?" would not have been asked if man was free to sin without fear of judgment against sin.

The awful complications of sin begin immediately, and they do not wait until after the act is committed; instead, complications begin to take effect when men begin to form the notion to willfully commit sin. Cain did not kill Abel out of a moment of emotion, as overcome with anger and out of control of his faculties. He used the very faculties of reason and thinking to plot how, when, and where he would kill Abel. God was not looking for the body; He was pronouncing judgment on premeditated murder. Today, millions of little babies in the womb are slain in just the same way. Their murder has been "plotted" as to how, when, and where. Even those who commit such terrible deeds without thinking, perhaps influenced by someone else, are not without guilt. They bear the judgment just as surely as one who reasoned it out and planned it, all the while knowing the full implications of it. God stated the full effect of the murder of one human being by another when He said, "...the voice of thy brother's blood crieth unto me from the ground." Cain was going to be sent away from God's Presence because of this great sin. There was nothing he could do to atone for it. As with every other murder that has taken place since then, the one who commits murder cannot atone for it in any way - no matter how agonizingly sorrowful he may be for having done it. Only the righteous Blood of Christ could take away the cry of Abel's blood for God's judgment against sin. He is the only Remedy that can take away God's holy wrath and anger against sin.

It is good to sing that old hymn, "What can wash away my sin? Nothing but the Blood of Jesus. What can make me whole again? Nothing but the Blood of Jesus."

Men Called Upon God

"And Adam knew his wife again; and she bore a son, and called his name Seth: For God, said she, hath appointed me another seed instead of Abel, whom Cain slew. And to Seth, to him also there was born a son; and he called his name Enos: then began men to call upon the name of the LORD." Genesis 4:25-26

Sometime after the loss of their sons - Abel by death, and Cain by separation at God's decree - Adam and Eve had another son and called his name Seth. The name meant, "substituted," showing that Seth was taking the place of their first two sons, now lost to them - especially Abel. Responsibility for the continuance of the human line from which the Promised One would come was upon Seth now. Eve may have wrongly thought that Cain was that one when at his birth she stated, "I have gotten a man from the LORD"; but now she realized that Seth was just a man. When Seth married and had a son, he named him Enos, which simply meant, "another man." Seth's and Enos' birth signaled the means of hope concerning the coming of the One God promised would be the Remedy for sin, but they now knew that any man born of Adam's bloodline was, "just another man." Such a man could not take away the curse of sin. They might not have understood exactly how the One who could take sin's curse away would come, but they did understand that He could not have Adam's blood coursing through his veins. It was after "just another man" came along, however, that men of this line began to have a sense of man's frail condition and their need for God's mercy and grace.

The Bible says very quietly and simply, "Then began men to call upon the name of the LORD." What did that mean? Did they call out to Him as they sensed His Presence among them? Some Bible commentators believe that this was the beginning of public worship. Others speculate that it meant something evil, concerning making idols and calling them by God's Name. The latter doesn't seem very likely, because they probably did not know what to call Him. The first time we are told that God spoke His Name was after the Flood, and then it was to Abram. " And he said unto him, I am the LORD that brought thee out of Ur of the Chaldees, to give thee this land to inherit it"

(Genesis 15:7). The fact that men began to call upon the Name of the Lord seems rather to show us that they called upon the Promised Redeemer, and while they might not have had a specific name to use, their calling upon the Lord shows that they placed their hope in the One God had promised would come. This is the same concept as described in the New Testament when Paul spoke to reassure new Christians of the validity of their hope being, "Christ in you, the hope of glory." That seems to be the motivating factor in men who began to call upon the name of the Lord. They had a hope of Christ, and they began to call upon the Lord within the bounds of that hope. The validity of our hope today is also bound up in the hope of Christ. We know by faith that He has come, and we know His name. When we pray, sing, or preach, we realize the One in whom our hope resides. Even though they did not yet know His name, the men who would later be called the sons of God, believed in Christ - the promised Redeemer - and called upon God from the standpoint of that belief. God has not changed. If you truly call upon the Name of the Lord, you are doing so from the same basis as were the men of Enos' day. The blessed difference is that we know He did come and He hath redeemed His people from the curse of Adam's sin.

It is good to thank God that we have been given power to call upon the Name of the Lord.

A Man Walked With God

"And Enoch walked with God: and he was not; for God took him." Genesis 5:24

In the seventh generation from Adam, a simple testimony of faith is given us: Enoch walked with God. Adam had once walked with God in the Garden of Eden, face to face, presence to Presence; now, here is the account of one of his heirs who walked with God. Why we are told this about Enoch is a mystery. He is the only man of whom this is said in all the generations from Adam to Noah. Was he the only one of this line who walked with God? Surely others served God. We are told even as far back as Enos' generation that men began to call upon the name of the Lord; but there was something special about Enoch. First, he lived the shortest length of time on the earth of any in the line from Adam to Noah. That is not what made him special, however; what made him special is that God took him. Where all others of Adam's line up to that point had the death of the body as a promised end, Enoch did not die. God took him. Why? We could speculate on that question for a long time, but that is not the most important point to consider or the lesson to be learned. What is most important is that Enoch walked with God.

How did a man of that era walk with God? We have said that Adam once walked with God face to face in the Garden. He "saw" Him, in a sense. He knew God was there with him in the Garden. Once the experience of the Garden was over, after Adam's great disobedience, that type of communion with God was impossible. Still, we're told that Enoch walked with God. The only way that was possible then is the same way it is possible today: Enoch walked by faith. The question is: faith in what? Or Whom? The obvious answer is faith in God. What was there about God that inspired faith in Enoch, though? What aspect of His character or what attribute of God inspires faith in a man? First of all, Enoch's faith was not merely inspiration, not just admiration. He did not manufacture faith from his natural abilities and then apply it to spiritual matters where God was concerned. What, then? The writer of the New Testament's Epistle to the Hebrews tells us that faith is wrapped up in a desire to please God. That same writer earlier proved that faith is the gift of God: not of works, lest any man should boast. How can one please God? Only by exercising that faith that God gives him, faith that is given for that purpose. In Hebrews we are told that in order to please God, a man must believe that He is, and that He is a rewarder of them that earnestly seek Him. How did Enoch walk with God? He believed that He is. Now the question becomes:

is what? He believed in the eternal nature of God, in His holiness and righteousness. If so, then Enoch believed in Christ. He walked with God in the full hope of a Redeemer, and he desired the "rewards" that can only come from a belief in an eternal, all-powerful Redeemer. He trusted in God. He believed God would do what He told Eve He would do; send a righteous man (Seed of the woman) to destroy sin. Without faith it is impossible to please God, but He provides that faith. Enoch walked in it, walked with God, and God rewarded him by taking him without his seeing death.

It is good to walk with God, just as Enoch did. We do not have the promise of being "taken" without suffering a natural death, but we do have the promise of great spiritual rewards as we walk with Him.

And He Died

"And all the days that Adam lived were nine hundred and thirty years: and he died." Genesis 5:5

Hundreds of years went by after God issued His judgment against Adam's sin and proclaimed the penalty of it, speaking of the coming disobedience of Adam, "In the day that thou eatest thereof, thou shalt surely die." Yet, Adam did not immediately die a natural death after God stated that his death would surely come. He died a death of separation from the pure joy he once enjoyed walking with God in the Garden. He died to the state of "innocence" in which he was created, meaning that, before Adam sinned, he did not know anything but good. All that was good was prepared and given to him by his Creator for his enjoyment, and Adam knew nothing else. After his disobedience, he could never again enjoy that good and pleasant communion he once had with God there in the Garden. That part of his existence was dead to him, and he lived for the majority of nine hundred-plus years under the conditions God prescribed for him as a result of his sin: toiling and tilling the ground by the sweat of his brow, struggling against the thorns and thistles that came because of his sin and tried to choke out what good he could scrape out of the ground by hard labor. For a good part of the time that he lived after his son Seth was born, Adam had many other sons and daughters born to him. These successive generations also lived long lives and begat many children; but we know nothing about them except that they lived, begat sons and daughters, and died. Natural death was the expected end of natural life, and even with such long lives as the norm, death was understood to be their end.

The Apostle Paul, speaking more of the fear of death than its actual occurrence, said in his letter to the Romans, "Wherefore, as by one man sin entered into the world, and death by sin; and so death passed upon all men, for that all have sinned: (For until the law sin was in the world: but sin is not imputed when there is no law. Nevertheless death reigned from Adam to Moses, even over them that had not sinned after the similitude of Adam's transgression, who is the figure of him that was to come" (Romans 5:12-14). Death passed upon all men, and death reigned. It reigned, Paul said, even over them that had not sinned after the similitude of Adam's transgression. Why did subsequent generations have to suffer the penalty of Adam's sin? They had not sinned after Adam, as in original sin; yet they inherited a sin nature in Adam that brought forth sin and death in each one. Not one natural heir with the bloodline of the father of all mankind has ever been guiltless, or without sin. Just as surely as every heir of Adam's has inherited the penalty of natural death as his end, so also has he inherited the consequence of death by sin. This would lead Paul to state a number of truths about man's inherited nature. "For all have sinned and come short of the glory of God," he said in Romans 3. In that same area of Scripture he would also say, "There is none righteous; no, not one." All are conceived with a sin nature that is dead to spiritual things, and are born to die a natural death. Adam did not die a natural death immediately, in fact, he lived until the generation just before Noah's - dieing during the life of Lamech, Noah's father and the ninth generation from Adam. Many, many sons and daughters were born to those nine generations of Adam's descendants, and every one lived under the same penalty: death. "For as in Adam all die," Paul would later say in I Corinthians 15. All that are Adam's - "in Adam" when he sinned - receive the same penalty. God, as it were, placed them in Adam from a sin standpoint. Thank God, however, that Paul added, "Even so, in Christ shall all be made alive." All that are Christ's - "in Christ" by God's grace - receive the pardon of sin based on the merit of Christ's satisfaction of the terms of God's penalty. Adam did not pay that penalty with his natural death, nor did his countless succeeding generations. Only Christ, the Seed of the Woman, was worthy to pay the sin debt; and He gladly did so for all that God placed in Him.

It is good to thank God for His amazing grace, whereby He has placed us "in Christ," and made us alive to spiritual blessings in the garden of His love.

Noah: A Man Who Found Grace

This Shall Be Our Rest

"And Lamech lived a hundred eighty and two years, and begot a son: And he called his name Noah, saying, This same shall comfort us concerning our work and toil of our hands, because of the ground which the LORD hath cursed." Genesis 5:28-29

Methuselah came after Enoch, and lived longer on the earth than any man before or since. Lamech was born to Methuselah, and 16 years after Lamech was born, Adam died. This must have made a deep impression on Lamech because when he had a son 166 years later, he named him Noah, meaning "rest." Did he believe Adam's death satisfied God's righteous anger against sin? His statement when he named Noah seems to indicate that something to that effect was on Lamech's mind: "And he called his name Noah, saying, This same shall comfort us concerning our work and toil of our hands, because of the ground which the LORD hath cursed." No doubt he had a hope that, if God was satisfied by Adam's death, perhaps the curse He had placed upon the ground for Adam's sake would be lifted. That would mean their lives would not have to be so hard, toiling by the sweat of their brow to scrape out a living from the earth. We should not fault Lamech for this. Every child born into the world is a token of hope to the continuance of life on the earth. Each new life holds the hope of being the

MEN OF LIKE PASSION

source of life getting better. There was also the hope that God's people had of the Promised One, the Redeemer. Maybe Lamech hoped that Noah was that One. He was not that One, but his birth signaled a far different end to the manner and mode of life the ten generations of Adam's family had known up to that time.

Rest. Noah was named and proclaimed to be the source of it by his father. The problem was that the earth was in turmoil, not because of the hardship of tilling the ground for necessary food, but because doing evil was rapidly becoming the way most people lived. We don't have to speculate what they were doing, God's word tells us that the sons of God - God's people - "saw the daughters of men that they were fair; and they took wives of all which they chose" (Genesis 6:2). In fact, the situation became so bad that, "...GOD saw that the wickedness of man was great in the earth, and that every imagination of the thoughts of his heart was only evil continually. And it repented the LORD that he had made man on the earth, and it grieved him at his heart" (Genesis 6:5-6). There was no rest for man. He did not seek it because true rest - the kind of rest Lamech hoped for when he named Noah - resides in trusting in and obeying God. The true Source of rest, the Lord Jesus Christ, would later say, "Come unto me, all ye that labor and are heavy laden, and I will give you rest." Man's condition during the time of Noah was, in fact, going to change the condition of the earth - just not as Lamech had hoped. Genesis 6:7 tells us, "And the LORD said, I will destroy man whom I have created from the face of the earth; both man, and beast, and the creeping thing, and the fowls of the air; for it repenteth me that I have made them." The earth was going to have a rest from evil, because God was going to destroy the earth, as men had known it. He would change the weather, alter the face of the earth, and cause great convulsions in the depths of the earth - all because of the evil men practiced. Noah's birth did not bring rest; but it did bring hope. Life would continue after God destroyed the earth, because, "Noah found grace in the eyes of the

Lord." Through Noah, human life would survive and the hope of the Redeemer would continue.

It is good to consider that Christ is our rest.

They Corrupted His Way

"The earth also was corrupt before God, and the earth was filled with violence. And God looked upon the earth, and, behold, it was corrupt; for all flesh had corrupted his way upon the earth. And God said unto Noah, The end of all flesh is come before me; for the earth is filled with violence through them; and, behold, I will destroy them with the earth." Genesis 6:11-13

The Lord revealed to Noah - who He declared to be a just man, and perfect in his generations - that He was going to destroy the earth and all flesh (including all humans besides Noah and his family) with the earth. Now, we know that he did not completely destroy the earth, and He made provision for humanity and the animal population to continue on the other side of the Flood; so what did God mean by the phrase, "behold, I will destroy them with the earth"? Was the earth an offense against God? True, it was now full of the seeds of thorns and thistles; but these things were an offense to man, not to God. In context, thorns and thistles are merely plants, and they operate like most other plants. It couldn't have been the natural earth that God found offensive; yet, His word tells us, "The earth also was corrupt before God, and the earth was filled with violence." The Geneva Bible notes say of this phrase, "Meaning, that all were given to the contempt of God, and oppression of their neighbours." It was not the earth that was corrupt in itself. Instead, all men had corrupted the earth by their wicked ways. What could have been pleasant to the eyes and fruitful in providing life's necessities was instead associated with man's corrupt nature and actions. There are still cases like that today. Our little town existed for over two hundred years without having liquor sold

◄ MEN OF LIKE PASSION

in it. Then, men began to push for allowing package stores and the sale of liquor by the drink. There should have been enough Christians to vote this down, but too many were silent. Now, our little town seems vile and wicked in my eyes. It does not even seem like home any more. The wickedness of man has a polluting effect on all things near him.

Even in the circumstances in which Adam and his heirs existed after his sin in the Garden of Eden, the earth was obviously productive. There was a gentle atmosphere on the earth that supported the growth of a numerous and varied plant life. A mist went up from the ground to water the earth (just as in the Garden); there were neither storms nor high winds to threaten. Even the animals God created lived in relative peace and did not even have to fear man. All that would change after the Flood. I have heard men speculate about how Noah would have to arrange the pairs of animals in the ark God commanded him to make, so that the flesh-eaters would not harm their natural prey - no lions eating antelope or crocodiles consuming helpless water buffaloes. I do not believe that was not necessary: all animals were plant eaters (herbivores) before the Flood. Only after the Flood would some become flesh eaters (carnivores.) The wickedness of man can be traced as the direct cause of many of the things we believe have always been in nature. Men corrupted the natural order of God (His way), and their tendency to corrupt whatever they touched and to choose evil over good was going to continue. What did God destroy in the Flood? Evil men? Unbelieving men? Yes. He destroyed them; but God also destroyed the order of nature that had made man's existence easier. Before the Flood there had been no rainstorms, no winds, plenty of plant life to provide food. God "destroyed" that type of natural surroundings. When the Flood came, it brought death to men all right; but it also brought great upheaval of the earth - all because of man's wickedness. Even though He was long suffering for 120 years after He said He would destroy the earth and all living things on the face of the earth, God judged that wickedness. How?

The Hebrew Epistle tells us, "By faith Noah, being warned of God of things not seen as yet, moved with fear, prepared an ark to the saving of his house; by the which he condemned the world, and became heir of the righteousness which is by faith."

It is good to remember that God will judge men's evil deeds.

Come into the Ark

"But with thee will I establish my covenant; and thou shalt come into the ark, thou, and thy sons, and thy wife, and thy sons' wives with thee. And of every living thing of all flesh, two of every sort shalt thou bring into the ark, to keep them alive with thee; they shall be male and female." Genesis 6:18-19

What a puzzle it must have been to Noah to have God command him to build an ark - a boat, when there had never been rain on the earth. Yet Noah obeyed. God was very plain about its purpose: the ark would save Noah and his household, as well as two of every living creature on the face of the earth. There was only one provision: Noah and his family were to come into the ark, and they were to bring the animals God commanded into the ark. The ark was salvation from sure destruction by the coming Flood. There was no other provision for salvation from the Flood's destruction, and the only proper place, the only place of peace, was in the ark. It was to be pitched on the inside and the outside so that the waters would not overwhelm it nor sink it. The ark was a floating vessel, moving along above the destructive depths of the waters of God's wrath. There were no lifeboats attached, no deck to walk along to enjoy the beautiful scenery, because outside of the ark was only death and destruction as the Flood waters rose and accomplished the will and purpose of God in judging the great sin and evil men had wrought in the earth as they "corrupted His way."

MEN OF LIKE PASSION

There is a popular saying that I have been hearing for a few years now, concerning the time Jesus came walking on the water to His disciples, who were in a storm-tossed ship in the midst of the sea. As He came near, Peter asked the Lord to bid him come to Jesus so he could walk on the water as well. The popular saying seems to admonish God's people that, if we are to be people of great faith, we must, as Peter, "get out of the boat." That sounds good, doesn't it? But when we consider that there was only One Who had power and authority over the wind and the waves - the Lord Jesus - we might look at this another way. Peter loved Jesus, but was Peter's proper place, his place of peace, to be found in walking on the storm-tossed sea? The only reason he could do so was that Jesus bade him come; and when Peter "took his eyes off Jesus," he began to sink. Remember, Jesus was not just out walking on the storm-tossed sea; He was coming to the place where his disciples were. Where was the best place for Peter to be? Was it not waiting for the Lord to get where he was - to stay in the ship? There was salvation in the ship. Remember when Paul was on the sea in a great storm and the Roman soldiers thought to kill the prisoners and abandon the ship? Where did the Lord tell Paul they must remain to be saved from the storm's destructive power? In the ship. In our day, the ship is the Church of Jesus Christ, which is the pillar and ground of the truth. Just as the ark was to Noah and his family, just as the ship could have been to Peter, and just as the ship was to Paul and his fellow travelers, the "Old Ship of Zion" sails above the waters of destruction. She is a floating vessel, moving along above the destructive depths of the waters of God's wrath. No, don't get out of the ship to try to show your great faith: stay in the ship. There is salvation there.

It is good to admire the beauty of God's Ship of Zion, provided for His people as a place of salvation.

The Rain Upon the Earth

In the six hundredth year of Noah's life, in the second month, the seventeenth day of the month, the same day were all the fountains of the great deep broken up, and the windows of heaven were opened. And the rain was upon the earth forty days and forty nights." Genesis 7:11-12

The Flood came. God said it would, and it did. Noah believed God and did what He told him to do: Noah built the ark, brought two of every animal into the ark for the re-population of the earth after the Flood waters receded, and brought his own family into the ark as well. Notice how Noah's actions showed he believed God would preserve him and his family, and preserve even the animals, exactly as He said He would. Unbelief may nod its head or speak words to pretend actions will follow that show it is really belief; but true belief always has actions attached to it. Noah, that preacher of righteousness, acted on what God said about what was going to happen, and what Noah needed to do to preserve his family. After Noah completed all the actions God required of him, God sent the Flood. Noah wasn't hurrying around trying to get done what he had forgotten to take care of or what he had put off. He was ready. All had been accomplished. The Bible says that, "in the selfsame day" that the rains began, "entered Noah, and Shem, and Ham, and Japheth, the sons of Noah, and Noah's wife, and the three wives of his sons with them, into the ark" (Genesis 7:13)

The rains came. These were not gentle spring rains; they weren't even the hard, driving rains we experience today. The fountains of the great deep were broken up and the windows of heaven were opened. Some scholars believe that a canopy of sorts - of water - permeated the "atmosphere" of the earth (hence, the "windows of heaven" were broken up), and a tremendous volume of water came down from above the earth. The fountains of the deep followed suit and great amounts of previously underground water now rushed to the surface of the earth. Whatever the turmoil, the waters came for forty days and forty nights, and the face of the earth was completely covered with water, up to a depth of "15 cubits" above the highest mountain. Every living thing outside the ark perished whose domain was on the face of the earth. The face of the earth was violently changed by the Floodwaters. All human, animal, and plant life drowned (although the seeds of the plants obviously survived.) The upheaval of the earth caused great mountains to arise, and formed equally great valleys. Creation scientists offer viable arguments for the formation of the Grand Canyon during the Flood. The planet's atmosphere changed from a "mist" going up from the face of the earth to water the earth to a violent series of high- and low-pressure systems causing storms and great winds. Atmospheric pressures caused by the Flood and the turmoil of the earth in bringing it about would remain after the Flood. Nothing on the face of the earth survived outside the ark; but all that God redeemed from the Flood's destruction were safely shut up in the ark, of which God was the architect and designer. Noah simply built the ark according to God's specifications, and the ark provided salvation - preservation from the Flood. Noah and his family and the animals went in before the Flood started, and the Lord shut the door. Noah truly found grace in the eyes of the Lord. God is also the Architect and Designer of eternal salvation, and none shall perish whom He has shut inside the vessel of His eternal Redemption, the Lord Jesus Christ.

It is good to thank God that you have "found grace" in His sight.

He Sent Forth the Dove

"And he stayed yet other seven days; and again he sent forth the dove out of the ark; And the dove came in to him in the evening; and, lo, in her mouth was an olive leaf plucked off: so Noah knew that the waters were abated from off the earth. And he stayed yet other seven days; and sent forth the dove; which returned not again unto him any more." Genesis 8:10-12

The Floodwaters continued on the earth for one hundred and fifty days after Noah and his family was safely shut in the ark. The Bible says that God "remembered Noah" and every living thing that was with him in the ark, "and God made a wind to pass over the earth, and the waters assuaged." The waters receded to the point that the ark actually rested on the top of Mount Ararat, which is in modern day Turkey. The only opening to the outside world Noah had was the small window in the top of the ark, and it was from that vantage point that he sent out first a raven and then a dove to test the condition of the world. He needed to ensure that the Flood waters had receded to the point of sustaining life on the earth once again before he removed the ark's covering and sent forth the pairs of animals God commanded him to preserve. First, Noah sent a raven, which is a bird that feeds off "carrion" or dead, rotting meat. This is not a pretty picture, but the earth, as it existed immediately after the Flood was not a pretty sight either. The raven found sufficient food, but it was all floating on the waters. He went back and forth from this carnage to the ark, until finally returning no more. This seemed to be a sign that the earth was becoming free of its covering of water. Still, Noah wanted further assurance, so he sent out the dove.

A dove does not eat meat, existing instead by eating vegetation. Noah knew that if the dove did not return, there was sufficient vegetation once again growing on the earth to sustain the other animals and his family as well. Just before the verses we are considering today, God's word tells us, "But the dove found no rest for the sole of her foot, and she returned unto him into the ark, for the waters were on the face of the whole earth: then he put forth his hand, and took her, and pulled her in unto him into the ark." Finding no rest for the sole of her feet meant that there were no branches upon which the dove could land so she could eat of the vegetation. One week later Noah sent out the dove again, and she returned again; but this time was different: in her mouth was an olive leaf she had obviously plucked off a living tree. This was proof to Noah that the dove had "found rest for the sole of her feet," and that meant the earth was once again a fit place for habitation. This prompted Noah to remove the covering of the ark and begin the process of re-populating the earth. The dove and olive branch have been used as tokens of peace since that very time, and the dove takes on special significance in the New Testament. When Jesus demanded baptism of John the Baptist, His obedience was given a special sign that He was the proof of the end of God's anger against sin, just as the dove and olive branch signified the end of God's anger after the Flood. "And Jesus, when he was baptized, went up straightway out of the water: and, lo, the heavens were opened unto him, and he saw the Spirit of God descending like a dove, and lighting upon him: And lo a voice from heaven, saying, This is my beloved Son, in whom I am well pleased" (Matthew 3:16-17). The dove was merely a sign of peace in Noah's day, but Jesus is truly our peace - and not just a sign of it. The "dove" found in Him a resting place for the sole of His feet.

It is good to thank God that His Spirit finds rest in the obedience of Jesus Christ, our Lord.

A Sweet Savor

"And the LORD smelled a sweet savor; and the LORD said in his heart, I will not again curse the ground any more for man's sake; for the imagination of man's heart is evil from his youth; neither will I again smite any more every thing living, as I have done. While the earth remaineth, seedtime and harvest, and cold and heat, and summer and winter, and day and night shall not cease." Genesis 8:21-22

The Floodwaters now being receded, the earth was once again fit for human and animal habitation. Immediately after God sent forth

NOAH: A MAN WHO FOUND GRACE

Noah and his family from the ark, Noah took of every "clean" beast that he had reserved on the ark and offered them to God as burnt offerings upon the altar Noah built explicitly for that purpose. These animals were not part of the pairs of every living animal (two-by-two) that Noah had taken on the ark at God's command: those were for the re-population of the earth with all manner of animals that God had created. Noah took the clean animals on the ark in faith, believing that God would preserve his life and provide the opportunity for Noah to offer up the sacrifices exactly as Noah was now doing. These animals were appropriate for this purpose because they were clean. Their being clean was more in the ceremonial sense, naturally; but in a spiritual sense, their cleanliness represented the fact that they were considered "holy," or separated for a holy purpose - as a sacrifice to God. Leviticus 11:1-3 tells us, "And the LORD spoke unto Moses and to Aaron, saying unto them, Speak unto the children of Israel, saying, These are the beasts which ye shall eat among all the beasts that are on the earth. Whatsoever parteth the hoof, and is cloven-footed, and cheweth the cud, among the beasts, that shall ye eat."

Noah understood the clean animals were for a holy purpose, to be offered as burnt offerings. The significance of a burnt offering was that it was to be considered as a substitute. The animal brought to the altar for this purpose was to be offered whole and completely consumed on the altar. Its role as a substitute may be clearly seen in that the clean animal was reckoned to be without sin and entirely acceptable to God as a substitute for the man who offered it, who is unclean as an heir of Adam and subject to sin. Noah and his family did not die in the Flood, even though the Lord had said He would destroy every living thing from off the face of the earth. "But Noah found grace in the eyes of the Lord." It may be more appropriate to say that grace found Noah, for that is exactly the operation of grace. It is typified in the burnt offering in that the animal losing its life is doing so as a substitute for the one who had the curse of death and whose death would have been entirely just. In Noah's case, the burnt offering showed

◂ MEN OF LIKE PASSION

that God had made a provision of grace for Noah and his family. The burnt offering was sacrificed to God to show that Noah's life had been spared via the redemptive value of the burnt offering. The animal died - albeit typically - for Noah, in his place. Every burnt offering ever offered pointed to the one burnt offering that would be the only offering truly able to act as a substitute - the Lord Jesus Christ. When Jesus died on the Cross He was the true Burnt Offering, without sin and entirely acceptable to God as a substitute for His people. Noah's burnt offering was acceptable based upon the merit of Jesus Christ as the true Burnt Offering for sin.

It is good to thank God for His provision of Grace for us.

The Tents of Shem

"And he said, Blessed be the LORD God of Shem; and Canaan shall be his servant. God shall enlarge Japheth, and he shall dwell in the tents of Shem; and Canaan shall be his servant. And Noah lived after the flood three hundred and fifty years. And all the days of Noah were nine hundred and fifty years: and he died." Genesis 9:26-29

Now that the effects of the Flood were behind them, Noah and his family settled into the new life they were to live. Noah became a husbandman, growing various plants including grapes in vineyards. God had commanded Noah and his heirs to go forth in the earth and once again populate the earth. Their existence was vastly different from what it had been before the Flood. Where before the earth's animals had nothing to fear from man, now the fear and dread of man was upon them, and God gave the animals to man for food. Before, they had only eaten "the green herb," but now God allowed them to slay and eat animals, saying, "Every moving thing that liveth shall be meat for you; even as the green herb have I given you all things" (Genesis 9:3). The Lord made a covenant with Noah and his sons signifying that He would never again destroy living things on the earth by a worldwide Flood, typifying the covenant with a rainbow. The whole human race would spring from Noah and his sons. Many years ago, I saw a chart noting some facts of anthropology where it showed that all humans fell into one of three major classes of people: Asiatic, Negroid, or Caucasian. This perfectly corresponds to the three sons of Noah: Shem, Ham, and Japheth. There are many races, but their roots can only be traced as Shemite (Semite), Hamite, or Japhethite. An East Indian friend of mine tells this story of when he first came to America. A person, who was told he was an "Indian," asked him what tribe he was from, thinking that he was an American Indian. His humorous answer was, " I'm a member of the tribe Christopher Columbus was looking for when he discovered America."

Here is one important point that God's word gives us concerning Shem and Japheth: God said He would "enlarge Japheth" and that he would "dwell in the tents of Shem." This was the first prophecy of the Gentiles - heirs of Japheth - being brought into the favor God was going to bestow on the Jews - heirs of Shem. Abraham, a Shemite, was the first person referred to as a Jew in God's word, and God bestowed great favor on him. From his line would come the Savior of all of God's people, and his son Isaac and grandson Jacob would receive the same promise. The sons of Jacob became known as the tribes of Israel, and the Lord Jesus Christ was born into the Israelite tribe of Judah - the Son of the virgin Mary. His fleshly lineage is traced back to Abraham in God's word to show the fulfillment of the promise God made to Abraham. From Abraham to Jesus Christ, the Jewish people were the only ones on earth to whom God revealed Himself in His Holy nature. Where all other people, if they acknowledged a higher power, worshiped many gods, Israel worshiped the One true God. They were told He was the God of Israel, and it was to them only that He revealed His righteous law. It was to them only that the mode and method of worship acceptable to the one true God was given. God revealed His Name, Jehovah, to them only. Yet, He had said that "Japheth," would "dwell in the tents of Shem." You and I have knowledge of God today because of this promise. We, as Gentiles, have received the promise that God made to Japheth. It was a spiritual promise rather than a natural one. God's chosen people in an earthly sense may have been the natural Children of Israel; but His chosen people in a spiritual sense included many more people than national Israel. When the Lord told Abraham that his seed would be more numerous that all the stars in the heavens, He was not referring to Abraham's natural seed. He was referring to his spiritual seed - the children of faith. That number comes from among all nations, kindreds, tongues, and families. We are now dwelling in the "spiritual" tents of Shem.

It is good to thank God for bringing His people into the "tents" (dwelling places) of the knowledge of His eternal love.

Abraham: A Man Who Was God's Friend

As the Lord Had Spoken

"So Abram departed, as the LORD had spoken unto him; and Lot went with him: and Abram was seventy and five years old when he departed out of Haran." Genesis 12:4

Following God can be an unsettling thing. By that I mean that He may lead us to leave the things in which we're settled - habits, places, ways of thinking, or comforts. Abram was, by our standards today, an old man; yet God would not let him stay settled. He had a purpose for Abram's life, and it was not going to happen where he had been comfortable. There were probably many reasons for that. God could have required Abram to leave the land of his nativity because it was a place of idolatry, and there is little doubt that people very close to Abram in Ur of the Chaldees were idol worshipers. The problem was that, when Abram left Ur, a good number of those people went with him - at least as far as Haran. We know this because Abram's father, Terah, died in Haran; and his brother Nahor settled there, probably because it was a comfortable place to practice his idolatry. We can know this because Abram's future grandson would make contact again with Nahor's son, who was still serving idols (Other gods. See Genesis 31:29-35). Abram would not settle there. God had a purpose for his life, and he was not going to leave Abram where he could have lived comfortably with idolatry all around him to fulfill that purpose. He had a better place for Abram.

What about Abram? Did he leave "kicking and screaming," as if he was going to obey God's call, but he really didn't want to do so? Not at all. As we first meet Abram we do not hear him speak at all. We hear the record of God speaking, of His calling Abram out of the darkness of idolatrous sin to go to a place later to be called the Land of Promise; but we don't hear from Abram by words. What we see is that Abram is a man of action. His actions do his talking for him here. How can we know Abram believed God? He immediately left Ur when God told him to leave. How can we know Abram trusted God? He left behind all that he had known - family, home, comforts, and familiar surroundings - to simply follow God. He had to follow him, because Abram did not know where God was leading him! The Lord simply said, "...Get thee out of thy country, and from thy kindred, and from thy father's house, unto a land that I will show thee" (Genesis 12:1), and Abram did as God commanded. Here is something that flies in the face of the modern concept of God pleading with people to do something: God did not plead with Abram. He commanded. Abram's will was not violated. First, God loved him enough not to leave him in the place of sin that was all around him. Second, God's purpose for Abram - born out of His love and grace - was not going to be thwarted by man's uninformed opinions: God has all the information! A verse that proves the power of His purpose and the goodness of His plans for us is, "Thy people shall be willing in the day of thy power, in the beauties of holiness from the womb of the morning: thou hast the dew of thy youth" (Psalm 110:3). Willingness to follow God in your heart is proof positive of the power of God at work. The next step is obedience.

May God's people see His power today, evidenced by our willingness to do what He commands us to do.

ABRAHAM: A MAN WHO WAS GOD'S FRIEND

There He Built an Altar

"And the LORD appeared unto Abram, and said, Unto thy seed will I give this land: and there built he an altar unto the LORD, who appeared unto him. And he removed from thence unto a mountain on the east of Bethel, and pitched his tent, having Bethel on the west, and Hai on the east: and there he built an altar unto the LORD, and called upon the name of the LORD." Genesis 12:7-8

"First things first," is a saying that teaches us to prioritize. It is something that we do naturally when our minds are not cluttered with too much information coupled with too much stress. When faced with a number of things to do, especially things that must be done in sequence, we will begin by saying, "First I must do this, then that, then that..." We know how to prioritize things. One of Abram's chief marks of a godly character was that he knew what to do first. When the Lord told him to leave his native land, Abram did not mentally run through all the things he had to do before he followed God's directions. He did not say, "I will follow you, Lord; but first, I must..." Do you remember some of the parables Jesus taught about following Him? In Luke's Gospel the Lord gave one lesson about what His disciples' first priority should be: "And he said unto another, Follow me. But he said, Lord, suffer me first to go and bury my father. Jesus said unto him, Let the dead bury their dead: but go thou and preach the kingdom of God. And another also said, Lord, I will follow thee; but let me first go bid them farewell, which are at home at my house. And Jesus said unto him, No man, having put his hand to the plow, and looking back, is fit for the kingdom of God" (Luke 9:59-62). Many times our priorities are misplaced, or rather established in the wrong order, and we fail to put God first. That is a hard statement, I understand; however, Jesus' statements above personally convict me. Perhaps they touch you as well.

After Abram followed God and entered the land of Canaan, he journeyed to a place called Sichem, unto the plain of Moreh. This was

49

going to be an important, symbolic spot of ground to Abram and his family for a long time to come. It was here that God first told him, "...Unto thy seed will I give this land." What an astounding thing for the Lord to say! Abram had no seed - no children. He was too old, and his wife Sarai was too old to bear children. The natural reaction might have been to think that God had lead him away from everything and everyone he had ever known to come to this place, only to tell him something that was impossible. Abram, however, was a man of "first things first." What did he do at that place, at that time? Did he sit down with Sarai and Lot to try to figure out what they ought to do next based on what God had just told Abram? No, "there built he an altar unto the LORD." Abram's first priority was to worship God by making a place where he could rightly offer a sacrifice to the Lord. He did not say, "Let's hurry on now; when we get to the next place we're going, we'll be sure to make time for the Lord there." First things were first with Abram. He consistently followed this pattern in his life, building an altar at the next place as well, where he, "...called upon the name of the LORD." What a wonderful example the Lord has given us to follow! Wherever we find ourselves, we need to decide what to do first - before we try to figure things out, or get our lives in order, or reach those other goals we have set for our lives. If we will set our priorities correctly we will follow the Lord, worship the Lord, and call upon the name of the Lord. Everything else will fall into its proper place then.

It is good for God's people to put first things first.

Down Into Egypt

"And there was a famine in the land: and Abram went down into Egypt to sojourn there; for the famine was grievous in the land." Genesis 12:10

Can the Lord furnish a table in the wilderness? Hundreds of years after Abram found himself in the middle of a famine in the Land of Canaan, his posterity would ask this question. It was not a rhetorical question one might ask to solicit a positive response; in fact, the very fact that the nation Israel would ask such a question was going to lead to serious consequences. "Yea, they spoke against God; they said, Can God furnish a table in the wilderness? Behold, he smote the rock, that the waters gushed out, and the streams overflowed; can he give bread also? can he provide flesh for his people? Therefore the LORD heard this, and was wroth: so a fire was kindled against Jacob, and anger also came up against Israel; Because they believed not in God, and trusted not in his salvation" (Psalm 78:19-22). The times were different and the circumstances were different, but the promises were the same. Israel failed to trust God's ability to provide while in the very process of being delivered from Egypt's bondage to inherit the land promised to Abram hundreds of years earlier. Abram was where God had told him to be, in the Promised Land; yet the natural circumstances in which he found himself confused Abram. The common thing for Canaanites to do when famine came to their land was to go where they could find ample food and water; but God had not promised the land to them - He had promised it to Abram.

Have you ever thought yourself to be doing what the Lord would have you do, but it seems everything is going wrong? As food and water became scarce in Canaan, Abram did what many others were doing, no doubt - he went down into Egypt. By the way, in much of God's word, Egypt is used as a type of being in sin's bondage. For all the things he did that seem wrong to us while there, such as having Sarai tell the Egyptians she was Abram's sister so they would not kill him to have her, the fact that Abram went down into Egypt "to sojourn there" is most telling. Can God overcome natural circumstances that seem impossible to us? He brought water out of solid rock! He created the heavens and the earth out of nothing! Can He not provide what we need to sustain our natural lives? I will not say that Abram did not trust God, but he did seem to lose his focus. One commentary on this event says this: ""Whilst the famine in Canaan was to teach Abram, that even in the promised land food and clothing come from the Lord and His blessing, he was to discover in Egypt that earthly craft is soon put to shame when dealing with the possessor of the power of this world, and that help and deliverance are to be found with the Lord alone, who can so smite the mightiest kings, that they cannot touch His chosen or do them harm" (Psalm 105:14-15).

Help and deliverance are to be found with the Lord alone.

Up Out of Egypt

"And Lot also, which went with Abram, had flocks, and herds, and tents. And the land was not able to bear them, that they might dwell together: for their substance was great, so that they could not dwell together." Genesis 13:5-6

We are not told what Abram's financial status was before he went down into Egypt, but we are told that upon his return to the Land of Promise that he was "very rich in cattle, in silver, and in gold" (Genesis 13:2). Not only was Abram now a rich man, but also Lot was also rich. God had apparently blessed Lot with a great increase while he was with Abram in Egypt. At first glance that might not seem to be a problem; after all, what can be wrong with having great riches? In this case there was quite a bit wrong with it. Where before Abram and Lot had been able to travel in the land of Canaan without alarming the inhabitants of the land, now they were conspicuous by their abundance of cattle, if for no other reason. Not only that, their herdsmen began to quarrel with one another, so Abram did the reasonable thing. He told Lot that they could not dwell together any longer, but Abram gave Lot first choice as to the place where he would take his family and his possessions. Abram wouldn't have lasted long in the rough and tumble world of business and the pursuit of wealth today would he? His decision did not make good business sense; after all,

ABRAHAM: A MAN WHO WAS GOD'S FRIEND

God had not promised the land to Lot, He had promised it to Abram. Many people might say that Abram was being foolish and unwise in making this offer to Lot, and their argument to that effect would only be strengthened by Lot's choice of the fertile plains of the southern end of the Jordan Valley.

Why was Abram willing to give Lot what seemed to be the choice spot to take his family and possessions? If we can grasp the answer to this mystery, we may be able to understand the faith of Abram; and if we can understand the faith of Abram we can model our exercise of faith after his. Why should we do so? We should do so because God blessed Abram abundantly. He was willing to take whatever portion of the land that Lot did not choose because he believed God. The promise of God was still in operation - He had told Abram that He would give the land to him and his seed. Abram may have faltered in his actions based on that promise, but God had never changed the promise. You and I would do well in our lives to trust what God has told us and act on that. Now, you might say, "God has never told me anything." That is just not true. He has given us His word, and in it are great and precious promises - some unconditional and some conditional. The unconditional promises are His work, His responsibility - their surety is not based on our belief and obedience. One such unconditional promise is that of eternal salvation. There are also many, many conditional promises that are based on our belief and obedience. Even the fact that God has based their surety on our actions does not make them of any less value. God's promises are sure and steadfast. We can make decisions with utmost confidence of their best end when we make them with full dependence on God's goodness, even those that seem to be decisions that will shortchange us where the things of this life are concerned. Abram was willing to shortchange himself because he knew God would never shortchange him. That is a pretty good way to live life, is it not?

◄ MEN OF LIKE PASSION

It is good when we are willing even to "suffer loss," if need be, to place our full dependence on God's plans and provisions for our lives.

Great Reassurance

"Then Abram removed his tent, and came and dwelt in the plain of Mamre, which is in Hebron, and built there an altar unto the LORD." Genesis 13:18

What does it benefit us when we obey God? He has been gracious to give us directions by which we may live our lives and simply rest in His eternal promises; but what about the here and now? Immediately after Abram allowed Lot to take whatever portion of the land he desired as they separated, God again spoke to Abram. This was apparently the first occasion of this since Abram went down into Egypt and "lost his focus." Now, back in the Promised Land, he had regained that focus and done the right thing to keep himself as a welcome stranger in the land. After having suffered what many might have called a loss by doing the right thing, Abram stood ready for direction as to the next step in his life. Many commentators say that is was only at this point that Abram stood perfectly in obedience to God's first command for him to leave the land of Ur and travel to the Land of Promise. After having separated himself from Lot and the last ties back to his former life, Abram stood unencumbered and able to move at God's command without having to consider what effect that might have on those who were dependent on him but were not part of the Promises he had from the Lord. It was then that God gave Abram great reassurance of the future and Abram once again responded by moving at God's directions.

Obedience yields great reassurance. It may not immediately yield the results one would desire, but obedience gives us the comfort and confidence that all is well and in God's hands. At least at that point we are willing to trust in His timetable for realizing the end of

His promises. For Abram, the reassurance came once again that the Lord would give him the fullness of the Land of Promise. "And the LORD said unto Abram, after that Lot was separated from him, Lift up now thine eyes, and look from the place where thou art northward, and southward, and eastward, and westward: For all the land which thou seest, to thee will I give it, and to thy seed forever. And I will make thy seed as the dust of the earth: so that if a man can number the dust of the earth, then shall thy seed also be numbered. Arise, walk through the land in the length of it and in the breadth of it; for I will give it unto thee" (Genesis 13:14-17). There were both natural and spiritual promises wrapped up in this great reassurance: first, Abram's natural seed would later come and possess the land Abram's feet would walk upon; second, it would be from the natural seed of Abram that the Savior of God's dear people would come; and third, a numberless throng of those who would exercise the same faith as faithful Abram exercised would be called (by faith) the children of faithful Abraham - as his name would later be called. What was Abram's response? Did he demand that God execute a deed of trust immediately so he could have proof of owning the land? No, he simply arose and walked through the land by faith, exactly as God directed him. Obedience yields great reassurance of God's promises!

It is good when we experience great reassurance by our obedience.

He Gave Him Tithes of All

"And Melchizedek king of Salem brought forth bread and wine: and he was the priest of the most high God. And he blessed him, and said, Blessed be Abram of the most high God, possessor of heaven and earth: And blessed be the most high God, which hath delivered thine enemies into thy hand. And he gave him tithes of all." Gen 14:18-20

◄ MEN OF LIKE PASSION

One of the most mysterious yet most telling portions of God's word is this passage of Scripture. The writer of the New Testament letter to the Hebrews would later use it to illustrate the eternal priesthood of Jesus Christ. Abram had just returned from rescuing Lot, who had been taken captive by a confederacy of five kings and their armies from his new home in the plains of Jordan. They not only defeated the king of Sodom, Lot's new found home, but they also obviously saw Lot's great wealth and wanted it; but when Abram received word of the situation he took his own "army" - his great household of servants - and pursued the five kings. Using great military tactics, he defeated them and returned Lot and all the plunder the five kings had collected from Lot and the defeated king of Sodom back to the land of Canaan. Under the rules of plunder, all the goods and persons Abram had retrieved were now his; but the man who would later be called the Friend of God was not going to keep that which belonged to someone else. The one thing he did, however, was to pay tithes of all of it to this mysterious character named Melchizedek.

King of Salem and priest of the most high God, these were the titles given to the man who came out to meet the victorious Abram with bread and wine. Melchizedek's position alone brings mystery to his appearance. The word Salem means peace, and he is referred to as the King of peace. Not only that, he was also referred to as the priest of the most high God. As such, he was authorized to receive offerings from God's people and offer them up to God on their behalf. The New Testament deepens the mystery, referring to him as one, "Without father, without mother, without descent, having neither beginning of days, nor end of life; but made like unto the Son of God; abideth a priest continually" (Hebrews 7:3). Abram recognized that this was God's representative, and gave him a tenth of the spoils - a tithe - to be offered up unto God. Here is the lesson for you and me. Lot's decision to go and dwell among what appeared to be great luxury and comfort did not provide the security he supposed it would. Others coveted what he had and went about to take it from him and to take even Lot and his family into bondage. That is the real promise the world's comforts and seeming security have for the child of God - loss of freedom to walk with God. Abram, who could have kept the spoils of war for himself, would not be burdened with that which he did not consider having come from God's provision for him in the land. He showed his understanding that all possessions belong to God when he returned a tenth of the spoils back through Melchizedek. All else he returned to their rightful owners so that others would never say that Abram became rich by his own strength and devices. Here is his testimony, and we might do well to adopt it for ourselves, "...I will not take from a thread even to a shoelatchet, and that I will not take any thing that is thine, lest thou shouldest say, I have made Abram rich" (Genesis 14:23).

I pray that God's riches may appeal to us more than the riches of Sodom.

Counted for Righteousness

"And he brought him forth abroad, and said, Look now toward heaven, and tell the stars, if thou be able to number them: and he said unto him, So shall thy seed be. And he believed in the LORD; and he counted it to him for righteousness." Gen 15:5-6

There is a pattern in God's word where, immediately after one of God's people has an experience of great victory, he experiences a let down. Elijah is one example, and Abram is another. Immediately after he experienced victory rescuing Lot, Abram apparently became greatly discouraged. God had promised him a seed to inherit the land, and Abram - already an old man - wasn't getting any younger. God appeared to him in a vision to remind Abram that the Lord was on his side. His plea to the Lord was, "...Lord GOD, what wilt thou give me, seeing I go childless, and the steward of my house is this Eliezer of Damascus? And Abram said, Behold, to me thou hast given no seed: and, lo, one born in my house is mine heir" (Genesis 15:2-3). Abram did not doubt God. He simply wondered when God's promises would come to fruition. Have you ever experienced this? Perhaps you have been burdened to pray for something and have received the assurance that it will take place, yet time marches on and you haven't seen the results yet. It is a natural thing to wonder, perhaps even to cry out, "How long, Lord? How long?" This is, in a fashion, what Abram was doing.

Here is a wonderful portrait of the long-suffering and merciful, compassionate God that Abram served, and that we serve. He has not changed. He had not changed His mind in Abram's case, and He will not change His mind in our case. For Abram, the Lord set up a situation where that He reinforced Abram's faith. Isn't that wonderful? He could have rightly said something to the effect of, "Stop whining, Abram! Didn't I say I would give you a seed?" Instead, the gracious God of Heaven and earth led Abram out into an open space where he could see the countless stars of God's Creation - this was God's handiwork, and done in His time - and He used them to illustrate His power to do for Abram what He said He would do. Number the stars if you can, the Lord challenged Abram, knowing that is impossible. Even if by some miracle Abram could have counted the stars he could see, there were numberless ones he could not see! Consider this when you wonder if God can do for you what you need done. He sees what you cannot see! In fact, He created all things, and knows the end from the beginning! Praise His name! In light of this strengthening of Abram's faith, he "believed in the LORD." This means that he fully invested himself and his future in God's hands. Can we do that? Of course we can! The question is, will we? Abram did, and the Lord "counted" (imputed) this "to him for righteousness." I believe this means that Abram experienced the joys of the righteousness of his seed - Jesus Christ - in his believing in Him! He was already a child of God, but it was in believing in the promises of Christ that he experienced righteousness, peace, and joy. So can we.

I pray that we may experience righteousness, peace, and joy - the kingdom of Christ - today.

The Future Declared

"And God said, Sarah thy wife shall bear thee a son indeed; and thou shalt call his name Isaac: and I will establish my covenant with him for an everlasting covenant, and with his seed after him." Gen 17:19

Waiting is a hard thing to do, especially when you do not know when the end of the wait will come. Have you ever been waiting for someone for so long that you decide to go looking for him or her, rather than wait for him or her to come to you? That is sort of what Abram did concerning God's promise to him that he would have a son. He wasn't alone in this; Sarai his wife decided to help him. She began to think that it was impossible for her to be a part of God's promise, so she gave her handmaid to Abram so that he could have a son by her. The problems that arose from her lack of patience still plague the heirs of Abraham today. Hagar bore a child called Ishmael with Abram, and despised Sarai's barren condition because of it. Ishmael would grow to be a great nation in his own right, but he was not the one who was the fulfillment of God's promise to Abram. In fact, the heirs of Ishmael and the heirs of the son through whom the spiritual promises would come are still at war today in the middle east. What a mess we make when we fail to wait on God! But what a merciful God we serve who will not allow our lack of patience and our self-will to negate His promises!

Rather than cast off Abram because of his hasty actions, God instead reassured him of His intentions to bless him richly. He did so first by changing Abram's name to Abraham, which meant father of a multitude. He further reinforced the strength of His promise by changing Sarai's name to Sarah, which meant wife of Abraham. By changing their names, he strengthened the bond of their marriage. At the same time He strengthened the bond of His covenant with Abraham by showing him that God's covenant was also with Isaac, who was not yet born. When God named Isaac before his birth, He gave His assurance that this would come to pass. God works the future in the past. He declares His purpose and the result of His promises before they come to pass. Just as surely as He spoke the name of one not yet born, so does He speak the name of every one of His dear children even before they are born. Take reassurance fro this: God knew you before you were ever born. Not just immediately before either. He knew you in the strength of His own declarations of the Promise of Salvation before He ever formed the world! In His Wisdom and Grace, you were declared to be the fulfillment of His promise even in eternity past. Just as surely as Isaac was called the Son of Promise, so is everyone chosen in Christ before the foundation of the world; and God is not going to allow the self-will or sinful nature of anyone of them to negate His Promise. So He did with Abraham, and so He still does with His people today.

I pray that we will be reassured today of our standing with the One Who declared our salvation before we were ever born!

Too Hard for the Lord?

"Is any thing too hard for the LORD? At the time appointed I will return unto thee, according to the time of life, and Sarah shall have a son." Genesis 18:14

As a ninety-year-old man, Abraham would once again receive confirmation of God's promise to him that he would have a son. The difference was in the way the confirmation was delivered and in the specific nature of the confirmation. To find out all one can about any subject, there are certain one-word questions that can be asked: who, what, where, how, and when? Once you know these things, you can have confidence in the information. Up to this point, the Lord had

ABRAHAM: A MAN WHO WAS GOD'S FRIEND

promised Abraham future blessings by going from a promise with few specifics to slowly revealing the answers to the one-word questions. What? The answer was that Abraham would have a seed to inherit the land God had promised him. Who? The Lord even told Abraham the name of his future son, Isaac. Where? Although not specifically stated, the sure implication was that the promise would be fulfilled in the Land of Promise. How? Not just in any way, nor by any means would this thing come to pass; because the Lord had specifically stated that Sarah would bear a son to Abraham. When? This was the hardest question. Several years had passed and still there was no specific answer to when God would make good on His promise - until this point in the ninety year old man's life. Here, under an oak tree in the plains of Mamre, Abraham would receive the final piece of information and, as the New Testament phrases it, receive the end - the target, the goal - of his faith.

Three men came by the place of Abraham's encampment, yet God's word tells us "And the LORD appeared unto him in the plains of Mamre." The number three is the key to understanding this, and it is the key to understanding all things concerning God. Surely these three men represented the three persons of the Godhead - the Father, Son, and Holy Spirit - and these three are One. The Lord appeared to Abraham. The Lord specifically stated the time for the fulfillment of His promise to Abraham. If you or I state that in nine months to one year we will definitely do anything we are fooling ourselves. We do not have the power to accurately predict what we will do because we have no power over the future. That is one area that is too hard for us; but is it too hard for the Lord? In fact, the real question for us is the same one asked of Sarah, who laughed in unbelief when she heard the confirmation that she indeed would bear Abraham a son: Is anything too hard for the Lord? Is there? Surely, if this promise was important enough for God in Three Persons to be represented there, then that ought to be proof enough that there is nothing too hard for the Lord. This is especially true when the fulfillment of specific promises

◄ MEN OF LIKE PASSION

is not only to bless the one to whom the promise is made, but is also to show the sovereign power of God to work all things after the counsel of His own will. Yes, God had promised to bless Abraham and He was going to do so; but by blessing Abraham, the Lord was also keeping a promise as old as mankind itself - the promise of a Redeemer of God's people. In fact, the promise was even older than that. The three in One Godhead, in counsel with Himself, established the Covenant of Redemption, purely by His grace, before the world began; then He created the world and man, setting in motion the fulfillment of His promise to save His people from their sins. In light of this, is anything too hard for the Lord? Sarah would soon see that the power and purpose of God to fulfill His promises couldn't be thwarted by natural circumstances. Nothing is too hard for His Almighty, Sovereign power to overcome!

I pray that God's people may realize today that His power and grace can overcome any obstacle.

Judge of All the Earth

"That be far from thee to do after this manner, to slay the righteous with the wicked: and that the righteous should be as the wicked, that be far from thee: Shall not the Judge of all the earth do right?" Genesis 18:25

Have you ever had someone ask you, "Do you trust me?" Even in circumstances when there is not much on the line, to fully trust someone else with your well being is a very hard thing to do. Now change the circumstance to one involving life or death. Let someone then ask you, "Do you trust me?" No matter how much you think the person asking the question is worthy of your trust, it is mind-boggling to think about fully, completely placing your life in another human being's hands. In the circumstance we're considering today, the Lord was not actually asking Abraham, "Do you trust me?" In fact, the Lord was allowing

ABRAHAM: A MAN WHO WAS GOD'S FRIEND

Abraham to potentially alter the consequences of His bringing judgment on the sinful cities of Sodom and Gomorrah. So great was their sin that the Lord had determined that He would destroy both cities and all who resided there. Do you remember who resided there? Abraham's nephew Lot and his family resided in Sodom; but the Lord was going to give Abraham the opportunity to intercede on Lot's behalf. Intercession is a wonderful thing, even when we do not realize that one is interceding on our behalf. Lot had no idea of what was about to happen. He had not been asked by anyone, "Do you trust me?" The Lord went to Abraham because He knew Abraham trusted Him. By the way, He knows whether you trust Him or not as well.

The Lord said a marvelous thing concerning His friend, Abraham. "And the LORD said, Shall I hide from Abraham that thing which I do; Seeing that Abraham shall surely become a great and mighty nation, and all the nations of the earth shall be blessed in him? For I know him, that he will command his children and his household after him, and they shall keep the way of the LORD, to do justice and judgment; that the LORD may bring upon Abraham that which he hath spoken of him" (Genesis 18:17-19). Once the Lord made known to Abraham what he was about to do, Abraham began to intercede for Lot and his family. The premise of his intercession was this: "...Wilt thou also destroy the righteous with the wicked?" (Genesis 18:23). Abraham began with certain numbers of the righteous, asking the Lord if He would spare the cities on their behalf. Fifty, forty-five, forty, thirty, twenty, and finally ten - Abraham "tested" the Lord's willingness to spare the cities on behalf of the righteous people He found there. Abraham trusted God, and the Lord knew it. In fact, his trust was best captured in the rhetorical question, Shall not the Judge of all the earth do right? What do you say? Shall He do right (or righteously)? First let's consider this: do you believe He is the Judge of all the earth? Do you trust Him to do righteously with that over which He is Judge? A dear minister friend of mine was new to the ministry and was struggling with giving himself full time to the gospel ministry and accepting a call to pastor a church far from his home. He had a good job, lived in the community where he had grown up, and had well-meaning friends counseling him to think twice about giving all that up. He agonized over the thing until the Lord brought this very Scripture to his mind, "Shall not the Judge of all the earth do right?" Did he trust the Lord, or not? Was he willing to place his and his family's life in God's hands and trust the outcome? It so happens that he was, and his testimony is that God was true to His promises. Abraham also believed this. Do you?

I pray that we may each one remember this question today, "Shall not the Judge of all the earth do right?" In remembering, may we hear the resounding answer of our faith," Indeed, He shall do right!"

God Remembered Abraham

"And it came to pass, when God destroyed the cities of the plain, that God remembered Abraham, and sent Lot out of the midst of the overthrow, when he overthrew the cities in the which Lot dwelt." Genesis 19:29

The concept of intercession is a wonderful Bible concept. There are many human concepts that may be called intercession, such as intervention; but to have one intercede on the behalf of others requires a number of factors that human concepts cannot guarantee. If I intervene for you, it means that I attempt to impose something of myself on your behalf to try to sway the outcome of a situation that you and I would like to see changed. When you have one who intercedes on your behalf, though, the outcome is never in question. Abraham interceded on behalf of those who were righteous in Sodom and Gomorrah, and the righteous were delivered from sure destruction. The phrase, "God remembered Abraham," is not intended to mean the God had forgotten what He promised Abraham, or that it had temporarily slipped His mind; instead, these words are meant to show the strength - the power - of intercession. God had promised to deliver the righteous - He gave His word - based on Abraham fervently interceding on their behalf. It was going to happen.

There is another proof that having an intercessor is a guarantee of God's promises being kept. As the angels of the Lord were hurrying Lot and his family out of Sodom as it faced imminent destruction, Lot became nervous about the destination they were taking, and asked to be allowed to go to another city, closer to Sodom. The angels granted his request, but showed that they were under direct command of God to deliver Lot before they destroyed Sodom. "Haste thee, escape thither; for I cannot do any thing till thou be come thither" (Genesis 19:22). While knowing Abraham's intercession points out a wonderful concept that resulted in Lot's physical delivery, the better thing we can know is that what it points out is that Jesus Christ is our Intercessor in spiritual matters. He is the guarantee of God's promise of eternal salvation being kept. Whether in the first application of eternal life or in the benefits it grants God's people each day, God remembers the sacrifice of His Son on our behalf. When some people are trying to commit a saying to memory, they write it down - on paper, on a mirror, on the back of their hand - so that it is readily available if it slips their mind. If you are one of those people, here is a good saying to write down, "We have an Intercessor with the Father." If you don't always remember that, don't worry; God remembers Jesus Christ, your Intercessor. Because of Him, all those He has made righteous shall be delivered from certain destruction.

I pray that we remember today that God remembers.

As He Had Spoken

"And the LORD visited Sarah as he had said, and the LORD did unto Sarah as he had spoken." Genesis 21:1

◄ MEN OF LIKE PASSION

Have you ever wanted something, prayed for it, even confidently expected it to happen - and then been greatly surprised when it came about? That must have surely been the case with Sarah. She wanted to bear Abraham a son, and she no doubt prayed about it. She had even received divine confirmation that it would happen; yet, Sarah was surprised when Isaac was born. That is the mystery to faith: man's nature will not allow him to believe in supernatural promises, or even in supernatural occurrences. Look at how many people are going about trying to prove the Bible is true by looking for natural proof! One of this nation's astronauts spent the last few years of his life trying to find Noah's ark on Mt. Ararat in modern-day Turkey. I am not trying to judge his motives, but I assume he thought it would help the faith of some to have concrete proof that what the Bible says happened back there thousands of years ago actually happened. It will not. It may shore up the doubts of nature, but it will never add one iota to faith to find some natural evidence to back up what God said happened. "Now faith is the substance of things hoped for, the evidence of things not seen" (Hebrews 11:). Your faith accepts what God says because your faith comes from Him. It is not a natural occurrence; faith is supernatural. No amount of evidence will help, nor is it needed, to increase your faith. Experiencing the end of your faith, however, does cause it to be strengthened. Such was Sarah's case.

God had said she would have a child, and He said it directly to her. She had heard Abraham recount God's promise of a son many times before and she no doubt understood that Abraham believed it would come from her; but she had not had the personal confirmation of God's word at that time. She doubted that it was possible. After all, there was no way naturally that she could be a part of making the promises of God come true. She knew that; and she was right. It would take a supernatural occurrence to overcome nature. That is exactly where God intervenes and overcomes nature in delivering on His promises. He is in charge of nature; nature is His creation. When the Lord had last spoken to Abraham confirming the promise of a son, He also spoke to Sarah and confirmed it. He also spoke of a specific time when the promise would be fulfilled. God can do that; time belongs to Him and He is in full control of it. The next time you think time is slipping away, remember this: God is not restricted by time. Instead he uses it exactly to bring about all aspects of His perfect will for our lives. Nothing is untimely with God; everything will take place, as He has spoken. That is exactly the evidence of how Isaac was born. Do you need to see Isaac's grave to believe he was born and lived? No! Your faith believes it because God's word says so. Sarah did not try to rationalize Isaac's birth by finding natural reasons why it was possible; instead, she believed God had overcome the natural with the supernatural. Only He can do that, and He does it exactly as He has spoken. The very fact that you have faith and believe this is evidence of supernatural work in your life!

I pray that we may praise God today for the supernatural deliverance of His promises.

The Rule of Fairness

"And Sarah saw the son of Hagar the Egyptian, which she had born unto Abraham, mocking. Wherefore she said unto Abraham, Cast out this bondwoman and her son: for the son of this bondwoman shall not be heir with my son, even with Isaac. And the thing was very grievous in Abraham's sight because of his son." Genesis 21:9-11

Have you ever questioned anything in the Bible? Do you see something that seems unfair or hard to understand and wonder why God would allow such a thing to happen? Here is an example that, on the surface, seems greatly unfair! Having born a son to Abraham, Sarah quickly became afraid that the son her bondmaid had born to Sarah's husband could assume the place of inheritance that she knew her son had been promised. Even though Sarah herself arranged the circumstances that resulted in Ishmael being born, she now demands that Abraham "cast out" the "bondwoman and her son." How unfair! How hard hearted this seems to be! Before we say that, however, we should consider this from two aspects: the historical and the heavenly.

From an historical perspective, this was often done. No matter what circumstances arose in a family there was a clear understanding of the rights of inheritance. The first-born son was considered the future "prince," or leader, of the family and he had the rights to all his father's inheritance. This was referred to as the birthright, and it was a valuable "commodity" to possess, especially in a family as rich as was Abraham's. Sarah did not want a child of Abraham's who was born "out of wedlock," so to speak, to inherit what her son ought to inherit. From a heavenly perspective, the Lord was going to use this to show the difference between the flesh and the spirit. Ishmael represents the flesh, and Isaac represents the spirit. One has to do with self-reliance and the other with reliance on the leadership of God through the Holy Spirit. The Apostle Paul clears up the matter in more than one place in the New Testament, such as in Romans 9:7-8, "Neither, because they are the seed of Abraham, are they all children: but, In Isaac shall thy seed be called. That is, They which are the children of the flesh, these are not the children of God: but the children of the promise are counted for the seed." Can we let it rest in God's hands when we don't understand? He works all things according to the counsel of His own will, and the result will always be fair and just!

I pray today that God's people may let fairness reside with God and trust Him in all things.

Willing to Offer His Son

"And they came to the place which God had told him of; and Abraham built an altar there, and laid the wood in order, and bound Isaac his son, and laid him on the altar upon the wood. And

ABRAHAM: A MAN WHO WAS GOD'S FRIEND

Abraham stretched forth his hand, and took the knife to slay his son." Genesis 22:9-10

Soon after the Lord had made good on His promise to Abraham by giving him a son, He called on Abraham to do something that I will never understand. God specified a place called Mt. Moriah, and He told Abraham to take Isaac there and offer him on an altar for a burnt offering. This is one of those Bible passages that the unbelieving world points to as a place they believe shows God to be a cruel player of hoaxes. He gives with one hand and takes away with the other, they will say. There could be nothing crueler than to ask a man to kill his only son to please God, they believe. Why would it take such a sacrifice to show God that Abraham believed in Him? The truth is that God was not going to require Abraham to slay Isaac; this test was not about God trying Abraham's faith to see how strong it was. Instead this test was for Abraham to be shown how great his faith was in God's solution to the matter. Did the Lord require a sacrifice from Abraham? He was willing to do whatever God required because Abraham understood that he only had what God had given him to begin with. If it pleased the Lord to take back Isaac, then so be it. Abraham understood that the Lord doeth all things well; besides, he believed God was able to raise Isaac from the dead (Abraham would say that he had received Isaac as from the dead in the first place - his birth being a supernatural miracle from God). So Abraham took the wood and fire with which to offer a burnt offering and he took Isaac, fully believing him to be the sacrifice God required.

The thing was that God was not going to require Isaac to be killed. That did not diminish the wonder of Abraham's faith and willingness to offer Isaac. He laid Isaac on the altar, raised the knife, and was poised to plunge it into his only son and take his life to please God. Why did the Lord stop Abraham? He did so for a number of reasons, not the least of which was that Isaac's death was not required to please God; in fact, his death could not have pleased the Lord, nor could it fulfill the just requirements typified by the process of offering a burnt sacrifice to God. That particular sacrifice was a sin sacrifice, offered to appease the wrath of God against sin; yet not one sacrifice of a human or an animal could satisfy God's judgment against sin. No matter how willing Abraham or any other person might be to try to make this satisfaction, it was going to require God Himself to do it. He was the only One qualified. Now let's get back to the unfair, the cruel request that some believe God required of Abraham to offer his only son - the son of promise. The same ones who might say this is cruel are probably unmoved by the fact that God was going to give His only Son to die on the Cross, shedding His perfect, sinless Blood to redeem God's people from their sins. He was going to satisfy His own judgment; only He could do so, and it was His perfect will to do so! The prophet Isaiah said a strange thing in Isaiah 53:10-11, "Yet it pleased the LORD to bruise him; he hath put him to grief: when thou shalt make his soul an offering for sin, he shall see his seed, he shall prolong his days, and the pleasure of the LORD shall prosper in his hand. He shall see of the travail of his soul, and shall be satisfied." Was that fair? Yes, it was exquisitely fair! It was altogether righteous and just! It was the ultimate act of grace and mercy! God was willing to offer His Son in an even stronger way than Abraham was willing to offer Isaac. He stopped Abraham from taking Isaac's life and then provided a substitute for Isaac's life - a ram caught in the thicket nearby. God the Father was going to offer His Son as the true substitute for you and for me. He was perfectly willing to do so because of His great love for His people.

How we ought to praise Him today for His mercy and grace! I pray that we will do so.

Made Sure for a Possession

"And after this, Abraham buried Sarah his wife in the cave of the field of Machpelah before Mamre: the same is Hebron in the land of

ABRAHAM: A MAN WHO WAS GOD'S FRIEND

Canaan. And the field, and the cave that is therein, were made sure unto Abraham for a possession of a burial place by the sons of Heth." Genesis 23:19-20

How much would it take to assure you that God's promises are true? How little would you be willing to settle for as a surety that what the Lord has said will come true? God promised Abraham that his seed would inherit the Land of Canaan, "as far as his eyes could see," and He did so more than once. Now, after the death of his beloved wife Sarah, Abraham needed that promise to come true. He wanted to bury his wife in the very land that God had promised. No wonder "the faith of Abraham" is such a strong theme in God's word! His confidence in the fulfillment of God's promises was so strong that he made another investment in the promise, so to speak. He was willing to commit the remains of his loved one to a place one inch of which he did not yet own! Abraham was willing to take possession of such a small part of the land that many people might say that it was not worth the effort; but his desire was to take what the Lord would grant him and, by doing so, show that his full trust was in God's provision.

Abraham first went to the current owners of the land, and asked them to sell him a place where he could bury Sarah. There are some things worth noting here if we desire to model our exercises of faith after Abraham's: first, he did not go boldly into the camp of the children of Heth and claim what was rightfully his. As he always did, Abraham conducted himself as a "pilgrim and a stranger" in the land. Had God promised him the land? Of course, He had. Did Abraham have every right to claim it for his own, to demand that the current owners give it up to him? Well, here is a place where much of modern religion may be somewhat confused today. Much is said about boldly claiming God's promises in the natural realm - about marching right in a demanding what is rightfully yours! What about God's will and God's timing? What about trusting in Him to deliver on His timescale according to His wisdom and knowledge? Abraham, fully trusting in

God's future provision of all the land, was willing to pay for the cave in the field of Machpelah; again, he invested himself in God's promises. This little piece of land, where eventually Abraham and Isaac would also be buried, became a beacon of hope for future generations of Abraham's people. So much so that Abraham's then future grandson Jacob's body would be carried up out of Egypt to take its rightful place in the little cave - waiting, as it were for the fulfillment of God's promise. What hope that gave God's people! All because Abraham was willing to take just a little token to show his faith in God's promises.

I pray that we may gain hope today that God's promises are true, and invest ourselves fully in whatever He provides.

His Angel Goes Before

"The LORD God of heaven, which took me from my father's house, and from the land of my kindred, and which spoke unto me, and that swore unto me, saying, Unto thy seed will I give this land; he shall send his angel before thee, and thou shalt take a wife unto my son from thence." Genesis 24:7

There were a number of times in Abraham's life of walking in the light of God's promises that he tried to arrange things to take place before God's time. He meant well, and perhaps he truly thought he needed to help the Lord. This was not one of those times. As he drew near what he knew was the end of his earthly existence, Abraham began to make arrangements to obtain a wife for his son. That was the custom of his culture and time - the father would choose a wife for his son. There were many reasons for doing so: first, he did so because the wisdom that usually comes with age is better than the wisdom that attends youth. The young make decisions based on far different criteria than do the aged. Abraham's main criterion was that he did not want Isaac to marry a Canaanite woman. Why?

ABRAHAM: A MAN WHO WAS GOD'S FRIEND

Knowing Abraham, I imagine one of the strong reasons was that he did not want one bit of the land God had promised Isaac to come into Isaac's possession by rights of dowry. In other words, from the benevolence of any Canaanite woman's father who could take credit for giving Isaac what God had already promised him. No, Abraham chose to bring a bride for Isaac from his native land, out of the ranks of his own family there. Because of his age, Abraham was going to send an ambassador to fetch the bride, his eldest and most trusted servant.

Eliezer, the man Abraham sent, was a good man. We can know this because he stood to inherit all of Abraham's earthly goods at one time; but he was a good steward - faithful - and desired the best for Abraham and Isaac. He entered into a covenant with Abraham that he would perform Abraham's will in the matter: no Canaanites - no strangers from the promises of God; only one from the family of Abraham would do. He agreed, but sought to understand the strength of the covenant. Abraham gave Eliezer assurance that this was God's business, and that He would do what was necessary to ensure the trip was successful. Here is a key point in this account as well as in the spiritual work of God "calling the Bride" He has chosen for His Son: God does not leave the work of eternal salvation up to man's will or whims. His wisdom is the wisdom of the ages and of eternity; He has chosen a Bride based upon His wisdom, purpose, and will. He will perform His will. Just as with ensuring the fulfillment of the natural promises to Abraham, so is God's will perfect in the fulfillment of His eternal covenant with Himself to save His people from their sins and to bring them into the body of Christ, which is described as the Bride of Christ. Abraham told Eliezer that the assurance of his succeeding in bringing a bride home for Isaac from among Abraham's people was that the Lord..."shall send his angel before thee, and thou shalt take a wife unto my son from thence." Abraham knew that this was God's work, and His work shall always be successful!

I pray that today we may see the full picture of God's purpose and will to save His people - to bring them into the fullness of covenant relationship with Him by way of "marriage" to His dear Son. What a joyous realization!

God Is in the Details

"And the man bowed down his head, and worshiped the LORD. And he said, Blessed be the LORD God of my master Abraham, who hath not left destitute my master of his mercy and his truth: I being in the way, the LORD led me to the house of my master's brethren." Genesis 24:26-27

When we follow after God's will, all things will eventually work for good in our lives. We have that assurance from God's word in the New Testament, "And we know that all things work together for good to them that love God, to them who are the called according to his purpose" (Romans 8:28). There is a reason that all things "work for good", and that is because God is doing the work, or working the details, or however you want to say it. In fact, immediately before Paul wrote verse 28 in the Roman Letter, he had said this in verse 27, " And he that searcheth the hearts knoweth what is the mind of the Spirit, because he maketh intercession for the saints according to the will of God." Doing the will of God always yields good - it may not yield earthly comfort, pleasure, or wealth; but it always yields ultimate good. Abraham's steward Eliezer had agreed to do the will of his master. He was a good and faithful steward of all that pertained to Abraham, including his faith. Abraham believed God's promises and Eliezer believed Abraham - but he also believed Abraham's God. If he was only being obedient for Abraham's sake, that would be commendable but it might not yield good results. Eliezer was ultimately obeying God's will in the matter of fetching a wife for Isaac from Abraham's native country of Mesopotamia.

Eliezer had asked the Lord for specific directions so that he might be assured he was following God's will in the matter. He asked for the maid who was the right choice to behave in a specific way so that he could recognize her, and it happened just as he asked. Rebekah, a great niece of Abraham, came to draw water at the well where Eliezer waited for the one to whom God had sent him. Before Eliezer even knew her identity, she graciously did what Eliezer had asked the Lord to direct her to do so he could recognize that his prayers were answered. When he saw how specifically gracious the Lord had been in answering his prayers and the desire of his master Abraham, Eliezer "...bowed down his head, and worshiped the LORD." He blessed the Lord God of his master Abraham and recognized that the Lord had lead him to the exact one He had chosen for Isaac. How wonderfully things work out when we follow God's will in the details of our lives! If Eliezer had taken it on himself to find a wife for Isaac based on his own criteria and best judgment, he could have wandered around for years and still not found the right one. It is also important that he gave God all the credit and glory for this. He could have taken on some of the credit for himself by attributing his finding Rebekah to his "good luck," or "keen sense of awareness," or "exquisite planning." Instead, Eliezer gave God all the credit for first choosing Rebekah, then leading him to find her. Notice here that God actually brought Rebekah to Eliezer and all he did was recognize that she was the one God chose. There is a popular saying in business, "the devil's in the details." I don't like that saying. I would rather acknowledge that the Lord is in the details, and He is. When we follow His will, the details will work out for our good.

I pray that today's details will reveal God's will at work; and that we will worship Him for it.

Humility in Willingness

"And Rebekah lifted up her eyes, and when she saw Isaac, she lighted off the camel. For she had said unto the servant, What man is this that

MEN OF LIKE PASSION

walketh in the field to meet us? And the servant had said, It is my master: therefore she took a veil, and covered herself." Genesis 24:64-65

Abraham's servant returned to his master a successful man. He had succeeded in his mission to fetch a wife for Abraham's son Isaac, and he came to present her to Isaac. It was not as if Eliezer had to use all of his cunning and powers of persuasion to get Rebekah to return with him. She was willing to come. She had a will, and she exercised it; no one forced her. Was it always her will to travel to Canaan and marry a distant cousin? That's not very likely is it? She had not always known about Isaac. She had no doubt heard of Abraham from her family, probably from her father. His father was Abraham's brother Nahor, who had also left Ur with Abraham but had settled in Haran. We don't know if the family had received word from Abraham over the years since they last saw him, but they knew he had continued to travel west from Haran; and they also knew that Abraham had continued to travel because God had spoken to him and directed Abraham to do so. Rebekah had heard about Abraham all right; but Eliezer filled in the missing details about Abraham. He was very likely a good storyteller, like most people in those times - not a liar, as we use the phrase sometimes, but a teller of history. That is how knowledge was passed from one family to another and from one generation to another. As Eliezer told of God's promises and blessings to Abraham, his words began to have a drawing power on Rebekah.

She was not merely curious, and she was not looking to share in Abraham's riches for her own gain. Rebekah was drawn to the promises of Abraham - not just any promise, but the best one; the promise that, "In thy seed shall all families of the earth be blessed." She wanted to be a part of that promise. Why? Let's look at it in its spiritual parallel for just a moment to try to understand her motive. Why does anyone leave behind a life previously filled with the pursuit of worldly, fleshly pleasures and comforts to follow the Lord? Why did those Galilean fishermen "straightway" leave their nets and follow Jesus when He called on them to do so? Was it superior intellect, or a good heart? Was it a resolution to "turn over a new leaf?" No, that is never enough. It may be enough for a little while, but it is never enough for the long run. It takes a supernatural, spiritual transformation to cause one to leave off natural pursuits to follow after and desire spiritual pursuits. The disciples of Jesus had been spiritually transformed - born again - or else they would have never followed Jesus as they did. Rebekah had also been spiritually transformed or else she would have never left her native country to go marry a man she had never seen. We have already said that Rebekah knew a little about Abraham from the accounts of others, but she knew absolutely nothing about Isaac from that source. Her desire was toward him because the Lord placed it in her heart to love Isaac before she had ever seen him. That is why she did not have to be persuaded to go. She went because of her love for Isaac. We can know that because she was glad to see him, and she wanted to present herself to him as a chaste virgin. Seeing Isaac walk across the field as she and Eliezer came near to Abraham's encampment, she made sure from Eliezer that this was indeed her future husband and waited to meet Isaac. Before he came to her she showed her true humility and desire to please her future husband: "she took a veil, and covered herself." John Gill's Commentary on this says she did so, "both out of modesty, and as a token of subjection to him: for the veil was put on when the bride was introduced to the bridegroom..." Equal to her willingness was her humility. By veiling herself, she showed herself subject to his will. Did that violate her will? No! Her will found its purpose in God's will for Isaac. She personified the Scripture that says, "Thy people shall be willing in the day of thy power." We see the fullness of the meshing of the two wills by the statement, "And Isaac brought her into his mother Sarah's tent, and took Rebekah, and she became his wife; and he loved her" (Genesis 24:67).

I pray that God's people may see today that He has made us willing to be subject to His divine will, and praise Him for it.

◄ MEN OF LIKE PASSION

A Godly Inheritance

"And Abraham gave all that he had unto Isaac." Genesis 25:5

Just before Abraham's death, he did something that he would probably be roundly criticized for today: he gave everything he had to his son Isaac. Did he not have other sons? Yes, besides Ishmael, Abraham had six other sons and several grandsons. He had remarried sometime after Sarah's death and his wife bore him these sons; but they were not the sons to whom - and through whom - God had made promises to Abraham concerning the Land of Promise and concerning the blessing in store for "all families of the earth." There was only one son who fulfilled God's immediate promise of blessings to Abraham and who typified God's future promise of blessings to Abraham's seed. All that Abraham had was Isaac's. If we can imagine a scene where Abraham's will was read and executed - before his death - we can visualize Isaac receiving his inheritance according to the terms of Abraham's will. Have you ever received anything as a result of someone naming you in his or her will? There are two requirements that had to have been met before you could receive your inheritance. First, the person who possessed the property, or whatever material item you would be granted, must have named you in the will while still in possession of the item or items - and a will always conveys something concrete, something tangible. Good will or best wishes do not have to be specified in a legal document, and neither does something that may or may not come into your possession eventually. No, the person who owns the thing to be conveyed to you must specify exactly what it is and what the conditions are - if any - of your being able to possess it. The second requirement for you to inherit a thing is that the person who willed it to you must have died. In Isaac's case, Abraham named him specifically; but Abraham was not yet dead. We can still understand this, however, if we "fast forward" a few centuries.

ABRAHAM: A MAN WHO WAS GOD'S FRIEND

Abraham had a right to choose Isaac to receive all he had because Isaac was his firstborn legal son, the son of his wife Sarah. Yet, Abraham did not choose Isaac for this reason; he chose him because God had chosen Isaac to be heir with Abraham of the same promises. (Isaac would later follow suit and choose his son Jacob as the next generation - and for the same reason, because God would choose Jacob.) We can rely on Scripture for proof of this: "By faith he sojourned in the land of promise, as in a strange country, dwelling in tabernacles with Isaac and Jacob, the heirs with him of the same promise" (Hebrews 11:9). Why do you think there are people still today who do not want to grant God the right to choose whom He will choose? His choice is always in perfect agreement with his divine will. Even though Abraham was not yet dead, Isaac received the inheritance - all Abraham had. What did he have? He had a promise. Now, someone will immediately say, "It is not legal; there must be something concrete willed to an heir and the person whose will it is must be dead." In this case, Abraham was simply a messenger of God's will concerning Isaac, in whom the true Seed would be called according to the flesh. Jesus Christ, Paul tells us in Galatians, was that Seed - the true fulfillment of God's Covenant with faithful Abraham, with Isaac, and with Jacob. Not only so, but the Covenant - the will - was legal through His death, not through Abraham's. Now, we see that through Christ, "all families on the earth" have been blessed. As the One named in the Will of His Father, Christ Jesus received all that the Father had; and what the Father gave Jesus was His people - all named in His will from before the foundation of the earth. That will was sealed and executed by the righteous death of Jesus Christ, and you and I are still reaping the benefits of His inheritance.

I pray that we may see the Wisdom of God in naming in His Will all who will receive eternal inheritance with Jesus Christ. Surely if Abraham had a right to choose Isaac, then God had an even greater, perfect right to choose whomsoever He willed.

◄ MEN OF LIKE PASSION

He Died in Faith

"The field which Abraham purchased of the sons of Hath: there was Abraham buried, and Sarah his wife." Genesis 25:10

This is the end of Abraham. That is probably what some of the people thought that watched Abraham's sons bury him in the only spot of the Land of Promise that Abraham had owned - a place of burial - a "final" resting place as such a spot is called. All of the promises that God had made to him were no good to him now, they probably thought. He was dead. But there was a difference in the death of Abraham: he died in faith. We know that because he is mentioned as having done so in the New Testament's great Faith Hall of Fame in Hebrews 11, where God's word tells us, "These all died in faith, not having received the promises, but having seen them afar off, and were persuaded of them, and embraced them, and confessed that they were strangers and pilgrims on the earth. For they that say such things declare plainly that they seek a country. And truly, if they had been mindful of that country from whence they came out, they might have had opportunity to have returned. But now they desire a better country, that is, a heavenly: wherefore God is not ashamed to be called their God: for he hath prepared for them a city" (Hebrews 11:13-16). What difference did it make that Abraham died in faith? The fact that he did not receive the promises would cause some people to say his faith was in vain; he did not receive all that God had promised. In saying this, they would have overlooked the great blessing of Abraham going from a state of having no children to having many, many children. He certainly received that promise! But the promise he did not receive naturally, he received spiritually by faith - the promise that his Seed would inherit the fullness of God's promises to Abraham.

You would think from many people's definition of faith today that it entails drawing up a list of things you want and believing just as hard as you can believe that you will receive those things; and if you don't receive them, well, your faith was just not strong enough! True faith is not so! The Scripture above shows the true "receipts" of faith. Those who "saw" God's promises afar off, were persuaded of them, and embraced them, received full spiritual assurance of their reality - and that was enough for them. Abraham did not follow God by faith to receive a "laundry list" of things he wanted; he simply followed God. He walked by faith, lived by faith, and died in faith. He lived and walked in the Land of Promise as a stranger and pilgrim - a sojourner - who never acted like it belonged to him. He "confessed" that he was a stranger and pilgrim on the earth, as should all who name the name of Christ. Adam Clarke, in his Commentary on the Bible says, "How many use these expressions, professing to be strangers and pilgrims here below, and yet the whole of their conduct, spirit, and attachments, show that they are perfectly at home! How little consideration and weight are in many of our professions, whether they relate to earth or heaven!" Do you believe your eternal abode is in heaven with God? If so, then you are also a stranger and pilgrim on the earth. How at home do you feel? Are you comfortable - do the comforts that the things of earth bring you appeal to you? Or, like Abraham, are you willing to walk here as a stranger and pilgrim, desiring spiritual comforts above any other? Abraham did not receive full natural comfort from God's promises, but he received full assurance of their reality in Christ - and died in faith.

I pray that we will once again see our position today as strangers and pilgrims on the earth. When we do that we will enjoy our citizenship in that "better country" of faith, as did Abraham.

Jacob: A Man of Deceit Whom God Loved

Two Nations - Two Manner of People

"And Isaac loved Esau, because he did eat of his venison: but Rebekah loved Jacob." Genesis 25:28

The sons of Isaac were fully-grown. They were twins, but they were as different as night and day. Esau was a rugged hunter who loved to pursue animals to provide meat for the family table. Jacob was more "domestic" in his pursuits. He would rather stay close to his father's camp and assist his mother with various tasks. The differences in these two men were not some recent development as we see the description of them in this passage. They had been like this from birth. There were marked differences in them. For instance, Isaac loved Esau, and Rebekah loved Jacob. This is not to say that Isaac did not love Jacob, or that Rebekah did not love Esau. The difference was in the fact that Isaac was an old man, who had a taste for what Esau provided - the venison yielded from Esau's hunting trips. Rebekah loved Jacob because he was "a plain man," one who stayed with the tents and kept the cattle. We can step back from this scene and speculate on what was right or wrong about this situation. We could condemn Isaac for showing preference for Esau, and we could also condemn Rebekah for showing preference for Jacob; but we need to understand more facts before we do this. Things are never as simple as they first seem to us.

◄ MEN OF LIKE PASSION

Let's skip Isaac's preference for Esau. We've already said he was an old man who loved the meat Esau provided for him. Let's concentrate on Rebecca's preference for Jacob. Where did this come from? Did she know something about Jacob that Isaac did not know? I would rather say that Isaac had forgotten what he knew about Jacob from the birth of his two sons. But Rebekah had not forgotten. Just as Isaac was the son of Promise to Abraham - and not Ishmael - so Jacob was to be the son of Promise to Isaac. Before her sons' birth God had spoken to Rebekah about this: "And the LORD said unto her, Two nations are in thy womb, and two manner of people shall be separated from thy bowels; and the one people shall be stronger than the other people; and the elder shall serve the younger" (Genesis 25:23). Now, here is where we can get into deep water if we try to apply human reasoning to this. Would the Lord actually say that one of the twins would be preferred above the other? It had to be that way. Only one of them could continue the godly line of Promise that would eventually lead to the blessed birth of our Savior, Jesus Christ. In the custom of that day, the son to receive pre-imminence would normally be the elder son. The younger would always serve him. But the word of the Lord stated that the elder would serve the younger, and Esau was born first. Rebekah believed God. She knew that Jacob was favored by God and Esau was not. In fact, the Apostle Paul gives us stronger language in the New Testament than does Moses in the Old Testament. In the Roman Epistle, Paul tells us that God had said, "(For the children being not yet born, neither having done any good or evil, that the purpose of God according to election might stand, not of works, but of him that calleth;) It was said unto her, The elder shall serve the younger. As it is written, Jacob have I loved, but Esau have I hated" (Romans 9:11-13). We shall explore this concept in future days; but for now let's just remember that Rebekah loved Jacob for Christ's sake, just as did God. He was the son of Promise. Esau was not. Shall we accuse God of being unjust? Paul went on to say in Verses 14-16, "What shall we say then? Is there unrighteousness with God? God forbid. For he saith to Moses, I will have mercy on whom I will have mercy, and I will have

JACOB: A MAN OF DECEIT WHOM GOD LOVED

compassion on whom I will have compassion. So then it is not of him that willeth, nor of him that runneth, but of God that showeth mercy."

It is good to thank God that His ways are not our ways, and His thoughts are not our thoughts. We can place our full trust in His good and merciful ways, even if we do not fully understand them.

The Supplanter

"And Jacob said, Sell me this day thy birthright. And Esau said, Behold, I am at the point to die: and what profit shall this birthright do to me?" Genesis 25:31-32

Esau was Isaac's eldest son, although a twin to Jacob. Born first, he had the right to receive his father's blessing of continuance and first honor in the family. This was a treasured position in most families of that day, and especially in this family. Not only did the rights of the firstborn entail natural blessings, but it also held great spiritual significance in this family. The first-born son of Isaac would carry on the promise of the natural lineage of the Messiah. Just as Isaac was said to be the son of Promise to Abraham, it naturally followed that Esau would be the son of Promise to Isaac. The only problem was that God does not restrict Himself to what naturally follows. That is a good thing for us to remember today as well. Just when we think we have everything all figured out naturally, God works supernaturally. He is not restricted by the natural, and He works all things according to His will and purpose. Esau was certainly a natural man. Those around the family might even have said that he was a natural successor to Isaac; but that was not God's plan.

As Esau and Jacob were being born, Jacob gave a sign of what would come later. Esau was already born first, but God's word tells us, " And after that came his brother out, and his hand took hold on Esau's heel; and his name was called Jacob" (Genesis 25:26). The very name

Jacob meant Supplanter - literally heel-catcher - one who deceives, defrauds, supplants another by tripping him up. What a name! But that was exactly what Jacob would do. Esau wearily came to him one day from hunting and desired to eat of the lentils Jacob had prepared. Jacob asked an outlandish price, one that you might suspect Esau would never consider, "Sell me this day thy birthright." What nonsense! Of course, the eldest son of Isaac would never consider selling the place of honor he held! But Esau did not honor the honor; he did not appreciate the position of blessing he held. He was willing to sell it just to satisfy the hunger of the moment. It sounds like he would have fit well in our day, does it not? We seem to be surrounded by those who are willing to "sell their birthright" to gain some momentary advantage. Esau's answer to Jacob showed him to be what the New Testament would later call him, a "profane person," when he said, "what profit shall this birthright do to me?" He traded the natural and spiritual blessings of Abraham and Isaac for a bowl of beans! His decision may have been of the moment, but the effects of his hasty action were long lasting. Even though the Lord intended Jacob to have the blessing, He did not cause Esau to despise the blessing. Even though He chose Jacob, He was not in any way the source of Esau's rejection. Esau did that himself. God's choice of one over another does not cause the one not chosen to reject Him - he does so because he has no desire toward God.

It is good to look beyond the natural and thank God for His supernatural dealings with us.

The Deceiver

"And his father Isaac said unto him, Come near now, and kiss me, my son. And he came near, and kissed him: and he smelled the smell of his raiment, and blessed him, and said, See, the smell of my son is as the smell of a field which the LORD hath blessed: Therefore God give thee of the dew of heaven, and the fatness of the earth, and plenty

JACOB: A MAN OF DECEIT WHOM GOD LOVED

of corn and wine: Let people serve thee, and nations bow down to thee: be lord over thy brethren, and let thy mother's sons bow down to thee: cursed be every one that curseth thee, and blessed be he that blesseth thee." Genesis 27:26-29

First Jacob convinced Esau to sell him his birthright, and then he deceived his father Isaac into actually completing the transaction. Does this seem like the right way to start a life of being the son of promise after Isaac, of continuing the godly line that would produce the Messiah in the flesh? Given that the Lord had told Rebekah that Jacob would be favored, and given that the New Testament tells us that God loved Jacob and hated Esau, are we supposed to excuse Jacob's behavior? Did he know he was doing the will of God all along? Does the end justify the means? These are all questions to be answered if we are to understand how the will of God is accomplished. There is a distinct line between God's will and man's actions. He does not move people around a checkerboard of life, as though they are merely pieces used to accomplish His end objectives - some to be sacrificed so as to advance others in line to be crowned as kings. God's will and purpose for His people is always true to His purity and righteousness, and He never incorporates deception as though it were a valid tool for accomplishing His will and purpose. He will use man's natural bent for being deceptive, however.

We cannot excuse Jacob's behavior, but neither can we set up a penalty for it and think that God did not exact that penalty. Later, we shall see that God favored Jacob, just as He told Rebekah He would. Everything to which Jacob set his hand prospered. God spoke to him and guided him. Isaac's blessing that Jacob "stole" from Esau came true. He had both riches and power. In fact, it was in Jacob that the small family line that sprang from Abraham would grow into a great nation. God's obvious blessings would be on Jacob for the rest of his life, even to the point of showing Isaac's blessing was also prophetic when he said, "cursed be every one that curseth thee, and blessed be he that blesseth thee." All of this was for the man known as the Supplanter and deceiver. Blessed though he was, Jacob's near future life - the life he would live as a deceiver and refugee from his own family and country - was not going to be easy. Perhaps we still cannot understand why God would use such a man as the continuation of the godly line. The only real answer is that He chose to do so. We can search all day long and never come up with a logical answer. Jacob's behavior and methods were in most ways no better than Esau's. The real difference is that Jacob loved and had respect unto the promises of God, and Esau did not. The lineage of the Messiah had no meaning to Esau. It meant everything to Jacob. Did the end justify his means - receiving the blessing in place of his brother? No, but for whatever his error was in the means he used, the end came about so that God's purpose according to election might stand. As for Jacob, he would spend the rest of his life being deceived in some heart-rending ways. God's word, as always, assigns the results when men follow their own means in God's business: "Be not deceived; God is not mocked: for whatsoever a man soweth, that shall he also reap" (Galatians 6:7).

It is good to begin sowing in righteousness and holiness, so that we may soon reap the harvest.

Sent Away

"And Isaac sent away Jacob: and he went to Padan-aram unto Laban, son of Bethuel the Syrian, the brother of Rebekah, Jacob's and Esau's mother." Genesis 28:5

Jacob, second born son of Isaac, obtained the blessing of the firstborn through deception, and Esau had to settle for his father's standard blessing. Isaac could not give Esau the blessing of the firstborn son, because Esau had sold his birthright to Jacob. He probably thought their little transaction was not valid, and that Isaac would in fact invalidate it and give Esau what was rightfully his. He underestimated his mother's resolve and his brother's willingness to deceive their father. Even though the New Testament letter to the Hebrews speaks of Esau bitterly weeping because of his loss, he did not let that soften his hatred for the deceiver Jacob and his desire for revenge. He made a vow against Jacob, one that his mother overheard. "And Esau hated Jacob because of the blessing wherewith his father blessed him: and Esau said in his heart, The days of mourning for my father are at hand; then will I slay my brother Jacob" (Genesis 27:41). Rebekah knew that Esau meant to fulfill his vow. He would wait until after Isaac died, after the required period of mourning for his father, and then he would kill Jacob. Rebekah had engineered all that had happened after Jacob's purchase of Esau's birthright, and she meant to finish the job. Jacob had to leave immediately, and she had to convince Isaac to send him away.

There is an old saying, "Oh, what a tangled web we weave when first we practice to deceive." Rebekah had a tangled web on her hands and she was going to weave at least one more section on that web. She told Jacob of Esau's intentions and she convinced Isaac that she was greatly grieved at Esau's choice of Canaanite wives and did not want Jacob to follow suit. He must go to her home country, Isaac told Jacob and his mother, so as to take a wife from among the daughters of Rebekah's brother Laban. As he sent Jacob - the son of promise - away from the Land of Promise, Isaac probably knew he would never see Jacob again. Once more, he blessed him. This time, however, his blessings were specific as to Jacob's lineage and place of being blessed. "And God Almighty bless thee, and make thee fruitful, and multiply thee, that thou mayest be a multitude of people; And give thee the blessing of Abraham, to thee, and to thy seed with thee; that thou mayest inherit the land wherein thou art a stranger, which God gave unto Abraham" (Genesis 28:3-4). Here was his return ticket home! God's blessings were not to be richly bestowed on Jacob anywhere else but in the Land of Promise. Jacob would prosper in Padan-Aram all right, but it was going to take much longer than he expected. Jacob would be the victim of a great deception by his uncle Laban, and the results of that deception would lead to a lifetime of trouble and deception for Jacob. Still, he had the birthright and Isaac's blessing signifying his eventual return to Canaan. Only one thing - or person - could stop him, and Esau had vowed to do just that. Here is a lesson for us: what God has blessed, no man can successfully curse! Hundreds of years later, an eastern seer named Balaam would utter these words while unsuccessfully trying to curse Israel, "He hath said, which heard the words of God, which saw the vision of the Almighty, falling into a trance, but having his eyes open: How goodly are thy tents, O Jacob, and thy tabernacles, O Israel!" (Numbers 24:5). Jacob was sent away in a weakened state, and his brother refused to bow down to him; but he would one day return in power and Esau would meet him in peace.

It is a good day to remember that no man can curse what the Lord blesses.

A Certain Place

"And Jacob went out from Beer-sheba, and went toward Haran. And he lighted upon a certain place, and tarried there all night, because the sun was set; and he took of the stones of that place, and put them for his pillows, and lay down in that place to sleep." Genesis 28:10-11

There are times and circumstances in life where all we can do is step back and marvel at the grace and mercy of God. We look at the circumstances and see where He would be perfectly justified to be ungracious and unmerciful; yet, in those very circumstances, He goes against all human reasoning and exercises immeasurable grace and mercy. One such occasion was when Jacob stole away from the threat of certain death at Esau's hands - after Jacob deceived his father into giving him the blessings of the firstborn son. He had supplanted his brother and deceived his father, and now he had to leave the very

JACOB: A MAN OF DECEIT WHOM GOD LOVED

land that God had promised to the seed of Abraham because of his actions. There seems to be no way anyone with a reasonable mind could think that Jacob could find any favor at all with God. He was completely unworthy of any favor, and he did not seem to care. In fact, he seemed to be heading farther away from any place in which God would bless him. The truth is that he was in the very place he needed to be in order to see the grace and mercy of God. He needed to be in a place where he would not give himself credit for being a pretty good fellow who deserved God's blessings, or who thought his own obedience was the cause of gaining favor with God. Yes, there was a certain place he needed to be, and that is exactly where Jacob found himself.

He lighted upon a certain place, God's word so beautifully states it. It was not a beautiful place naturally speaking, and Jacob was not in a very good place mentally or psychologically. He was distressed at his condition and physically tired from the journey, and he lay down in the wilderness to rest with only a stone for a pillow. Here it was that God would reveal His glory to Jacob. In fact, what happened next goes against the pattern that most people have been taught in our day - that if a person will seek God, then He will meet them halfway and be able to help them. How limiting that is to the awesome power and majesty of God! His word tells the truth about Jacob's situation and God's power in it. "He found him in a desert land, and in the waste howling wilderness; he led him about, he instructed him, he kept him as the apple of his eye" (Deuteronomy 32:10). In the very place you and I might have justifiably condemned Jacob for his supplanting and deceiving ways, God Almighty showed him His glory, instructed Him, and kept him - as the apple of His eye! He showed Jacob a great scene of future blessings, and reinforced the covenant relationship that God had instituted with Abraham - the Promise of the Messiah. He showed Jacob that he was also a part of that covenant relationship, not based on his belief or obedience, but based on the grace and mercy of God. That is the only hope Jacob had, and it was a great hope. The hope of Christ is the only hope you and I can have, and it is also a great hope! If you have it, it is because God also found you in a waste howling wilderness of sin, and led you about, instructed you, and keeps you as the apple of His eye! God's grace and mercy are so immeasurably wonderful, so undeserved; yet, in places where all we can know is uncertainty, He leads us to His certain place, just as He did Jacob.

It is good to praise the glory of His grace in providing His people a certain place.

Behold a Ladder

"And he dreamed, and behold a ladder set up on the earth, and the top of it reached to heaven: and behold the angels of God ascending and descending on it. And, behold, the LORD stood above it, and said, I am the LORD God of Abraham thy father, and the God of Isaac: the land whereon thou liest, to thee will I give it, and to thy seed;" Genesis 28:12-13

Jacob dreamed. This seems almost impossible to believe since he was sleeping out under the stars with only a stone for a pillow. It would be easier to believe that he tossed and turned, hardly sleeping at all; or that he slept with one eye open. Under the circumstances, he probably ought to have tried to stay awake all night. After all, Esau had sworn to kill him, and he might have been right behind Jacob. Whether it was extreme fatigue or something else that caused it, Jacob slept soundly enough to dream; and, in his dream, God showed Jacob a great scene of future glory. In what most children learn to refer to as, "Jacob's ladder," the Lord revealed a wondrous scene. Jacob saw a ladder set up on the earth, and the top of it reached to heaven. Whatever this represented, it had its highest part in heaven and its lowest part on the earth. The language is specific that the ladder was "set up" on the earth. What was the ladder's purpose? Surely it was functional, since a ladder was not commonly used for ornamental purposes. It seems that this ladder provided a means for moving someone - in fact, the angels of God - from earth to heaven and from heaven to earth. The one thing we can be sure of is that the Lord "stood above it," showing that He was the focus of the heavenly destination that the ladder provided. We might stay puzzled had Jesus not given us a clue as to what, rather Whom, the ladder represented.

In John's Gospel, Jesus spoke to a man named Nathanael and gave a parallel passage to this one in Genesis, "And he saith unto him, Verily, verily, I say unto you, Hereafter ye shall see heaven open, and the angels of God ascending and descending upon the Son of man" (John 1:51). He spoke of Himself, and he used the parallel in such a way that there is little doubt Nathanael understood that Jesus spoke of the same scene Jacob saw centuries before. The ladder Jacob saw in his dream represented Christ, set up on the earth yet reaching to heaven. More particularly, the ladder represented His kingdom of righteousness, peace, and joy - a spiritual kingdom - established "on the earth," and reaching to heaven. His angels - all ministering spirits sent forth to minister unto them that shall be heirs of salvation - first ascend, then descend on that ladder. What a scene Jacob saw! Not only would his Seed - the Lord, Jesus Christ - fulfill the promises made to Abraham and Isaac, but He also was the promised fulfillment of the continuation of those promises to Jacob. As the Lord 'stood above" this ladder, He proclaimed His covenant with Jacob: "I am the LORD God of Abraham thy father, and the God of Isaac: the land whereon thou liest, to thee will I give it, and to thy seed;" Jacob, the Supplanter and deceiver was to be the recipient of God's immeasurable grace. He did not deserve it, yet God chose him to receive its blessings. So is our case. We do not deserve the ministering effect of the angels of God in our lives, but He has established the means of "transport" for them to ascend from earth to heaven and descend from heaven to earth. The ladder upon which they travel is Christ - the Seed of Jacob, and the Savior of His people.

It is good to thank God for His ministering spirits, who ascend and descend on the merit of Christ's finished work of salvation.

The Lord Is in This Place

"And Jacob awaked out of his sleep, and he said, Surely the LORD is in this place; and I knew it not. And he was afraid, and said, How dreadful is this place! this is none other but the house of God, and this is the gate of heaven." Genesis 28:16-17

There are some people who say they never dream. For those who dream regularly this seems strange, because they seem to spend their sleeping hours wrestling with situations and scenes that are at once curious and disturbing. Jacob was a dreamer - not a daydreamer, but one who, at least this once, saw images too wonderful and too disturbing for his understanding. He had seen the wonderful image of a mediator between heaven and earth, typified by a ladder upon which the angels of God ascended and descended. He had heard the voice of Almighty God reaffirm with him the covenant of the seed of Abraham. The Lord had confirmed that he would give Jacob and his seed all He had promised Abraham and his seed. The Lord had promised His Presence would lead, guide, and direct Jacob wherever he went: "And, behold, I am with thee, and will keep thee in all places whither thou goest, and will bring thee again into this land; for I will not leave thee, until I have done that which I have spoken to thee of" (Genesis 28:15). The promise of eventually being brought back into the Land of Promise must have seemed remarkable to Jacob, especially since he knew that Esau would never abandon his threat of killing Jacob for stealing Isaac's blessing for his firstborn son. Still, as he awoke, Jacob had a sense that his dream was not just the result of his mind trying to work through the circumstances of his life - Jacob's dream was real, and it represented a door of opportunity opening for him that would change his life forever.

JACOB: A MAN OF DECEIT WHOM GOD LOVED

Jacob's first recognition of the reality of the dream he had was to confess that, "Surely the LORD is in this place." How did he sense God's Presence? Natural senses can fool us; so it was not through one of the five senses - sight, smell, hearing, touching, tasting - that Jacob knew God was present with him. The way Jacob sensed God's Presence then is the same way we sense His Presence with us today: He leads us to a certain place - spiritually - and reveals the Covenant of Christ in us (the hope of glory). That is why Jacob was sure. He could not likely have explained why he was so sure, but his words convey that he indeed was positive about at least two categories of things: the reality of God's Presence, and the holiness of the place in which He reveals Himself. There is a phrase used by some people - less frequently today than in days past - to speak about a place that is dear to them. This phrase is used to describe a place of great spiritual blessing and comfort when people say, "This is Bethel spot to me." Why call it a Bethel spot? The reason has to do with Jacob's understanding that The Lord was in that place, a certain place, where he dreamed his marvelous dream of a mediator between heaven and earth. Of this place Jacob said, "How dreadful is this place! this is none other but the house of God, and this is the gate of heaven." The place became known as Beth-El (Bethel), which means, "The House of God." The Lord revealed to Jacob that His place was there, and He would bring Jacob back to that very place. It became so precious to Jacob that he immediately said, "...this is the gate of heaven." What a wonderful reassurance God gave Jacob! How often He gives us the same reassurance - that He is with us and that He will bring us back to the place of sweet communion with his Presence! This promise became Jacob's great hope, and it ought also to be ours - not that we will be returned to some physical location, but that we will be lead by God into the fullness of joy to be found in His Presence.

It is good to desire to be drawn once again to Bethel - the place of His Presence with us.

◄ MEN OF LIKE PASSION

Jacob Loved Rachel

"And Laban said unto Jacob, Because thou art my brother, shouldest thou therefore serve me for naught? tell me, what shall thy wages be? And Laban had two daughters: the name of the elder was Leah, and the name of the younger was Rachel. Leah was tender eyed; but Rachel was beautiful and well favored. And Jacob loved Rachel; and said, I will serve thee seven years for Rachel thy younger daughter." Genesis 29:15-18

Reaching Haran where his mother had sent him - to the place where he could find her people - Jacob found a most pleasant sight at the town well. He knew that this was a place people would eventually gather and where he could gather information about Laban, his mother's brother. Shepherds were at the well with their flocks, waiting for others with equal rights to the water to come so the stone over the well's opening could be rolled away. When all had gathered there at the end of each day, they would roll the stone from the well and water their flocks. Jacob asked the shepherds about Laban. "He is well," they told him. This confirmed to Jacob that he was in the right place. The shepherds then pointed out the approaching herds that belonged to Laban, being driven by Laban's youngest daughter. When Jacob saw Rachel approaching, he was greatly affected. He rolled the stone away and watered Laban's flock himself. Having finished this task, he then "...kissed Rachel, and lifted up his voice, and wept." Jacob told Rachel who he was, Rebekah's son, and she ran to tell her father. Obviously, Jacob fell in love with Rachel the first time he laid eyes on her. She became the object of his affection and he was willing to pay any price to claim her as his bride.

Jacob's uncle Laban was no doubt a man who knew a good source of free labor when he saw one. Knowing his sister Rebekah had sent Jacob to him, Laban decided to put him to work; but he knew that Jacob would be more likely to stay a longer time if he "received wages" for his labor.

Laban told Jacob to name his wages, knowing Jacob was infatuated with Rachel. Jacob then spoke the words that would tie him to Laban for the next fourteen years, saying "I will serve thee seven years for Rachel thy younger daughter." Why would he give up seven years of his life just to gain a bride? The answer is simple, yet it describes the loftiest ideals of the relationship between a man and a woman: "Jacob loved Rachel." It was no more complex than that, and yet that statement is the most complex statement ever made, whether describing the love of a man for a woman or the love of Christ for His Bride, the Church: He loved her. No amount of analysis will yield a better answer, for there is no better answer. The simple fact that a man loves a woman, or that Christ loves His Bride, is so deep that there is no understanding it. That love - when true - is based on unexplainable factors. It is not based on any condition, any merit, found in the object of that love. Even though the Bible tells us that Rachel was beautiful and well favored, Jacob did not love her because of that. Others who looked at Rachel may not have even used those terms to describe her; but to Jacob she was beautiful and well favored. Love is the sweetest fragrance, the finest apparel that has ever existed. Where love exists - the kind that Jacob had for Rachel - everything around the object of that love is beautiful. Jacob served Laban for Rachel. He loved her and he was willing to pay the price Laban required to gain her. Even greater is the love our Lord has for His Bride, comprised of each one for whom He died. He loved us and He was willing to pay the price required to take us unto Himself.

It is good to praise Christ for His love for His Bride, the Church - made up of all the elect and redeemed of God.

Blessed for Jacob's Sake

"And it came to pass, when Rachel had born Joseph, that Jacob said unto Laban, Send me away, that I may go unto mine own place, and to my country. Give me my wives and my children, for whom I have served thee, and let me go: for thou knowest my service which I have done thee. And Laban said unto him, I pray thee, if I have found favor in thine eyes, tarry: for I have learned by experience that the LORD hath blessed me for thy sake." Genesis 30:25-27

For seven years Jacob served his father-in-law Laban, working to "pay" him for his daughter Rachel. Jacob had been deceived in his first period of service and received Leah instead of the promised Rachel. He agreed to work another seven years for Rachel and willingly did so. During that time, the Lord blessed Jacob with eleven sons, Joseph being the last born into the family but the first born of Rachel. Up until that time, she had been barren; but Leah had been very fruitful. She had borne Jacob six sons and one daughter. It would be her firstborn son Reuben who would be in line for the family preeminence, according to custom; but it would actually be her fourth born son, Judah, who would receive the blessing of the firstborn son. And it would be through the tribe of Judah that the Messiah would come. Jacob's other children were born of Rachel's maidservant, Bilhah, and then of Leah's maidservant, Zilpah. In later years, Rachel would bear another son - Jacob's final son - Benjamin. But for now, he had a large family, and he wanted to take his family back to the land of his birth, the Land of Promise.

Knowing his father-in-law Laban's nature, Jacob approached him by reminding Laban that he had fulfilled all the requirements set by Laban for his daughters. There was no legal obligation left for Jacob to complete, but Laban was not going to let Jacob go so easily. First, he still thought of Jacob's little band as being part of his property, as was the custom of that day. He did not want to give up the potential of having Jacob's sons - his grandsons - available to work for him for many years to come. Second, Laban had seen that the Lord had blessed him, as he said, for Jacob's sake. He was treating this as an asset he did not want to lose, not knowing that the blessing was to Jacob, and Laban was simply standing close enough to gather some effects from it. That is the way the world at large is blessed, and that is the way America is blessed today. Make no mistake, our nation has been blessed; but not for the reason most people think. America is not God's favored country above all countries. He has blessed her for His people's sake. He has blessed her for the sake of His church in the earth, and if He ever withdraws His blessings from the visible church that still exists in this country, America will no longer be blessed. In that sense, she is "standing close enough" to gather some effects from God blessing His people. Laban did not care a whit for the spiritual aspects of God blessing Jacob; he wanted the natural fallout from such blessings. Likewise, the world does not care a whit about the spiritual things of God; but they want the natural blessings that attend such spiritual blessings. Laban did not want the best for Jacob and his family - he wanted what he thought was best for Laban. He would try once more to squeeze the profitability out of additional use of Jacob's labor; but this time, the Lord made sure Jacob received all the profits! God does not simply stand by and let His people suffer wrong at the hands of the world, and He would not do so in the matter between Jacob and Laban.

It is good to realize that the Lord is on the side of right and fights against the wrong. We can rest assured of that.

I Will Be With Thee

"And Jacob beheld the countenance of Laban, and, behold, it was not toward him as before. And the LORD said unto Jacob, Return unto the land of thy fathers, and to thy kindred; and I will be with thee. " Genesis 31:2-3

Jacob grew rich in cattle, and he did so at Laban's expense. The Lord helped Jacob to be paid for all the years he had worked for Laban without any pay. Through a system of breeding and cross-breeding certain types of cattle Laban had agreed to give him from his herds, Jacob was able to accumulate great numbers of cattle and Laban's

MEN OF LIKE PASSION

herds became thinner and thinner. Laban's sons took notice and became suspicious of Jacob; then Laban began to look on Jacob with distrust. Earlier, Laban felt he had great power over Jacob and could persuade him to work for basically nothing because Jacob was in need; but now Jacob was gaining power over Laban. Any time a man begins to turn the tables on another who seeks to manipulate his weakness, there is trouble brewing. Jacob was no longer the poor little nephew who needed a place to stay and was willing to work years for Laban just to be able to marry his daughter. In fact, the Bible tells us, "And the man increased exceedingly, and had much cattle, and maidservants, and menservants, and camels, and asses" (Genesis 30:43).

The Lord uses many means to bring about His ultimate purpose. Here it seems he used Laban's jealousy of Jacob and the potential for trouble between the two men. Jacob was now as powerful as Laban, and Laban would eventually find out how Jacob had tricked Laban into giving him the start of his plan to breed goats that would belong to Jacob - those "spotted and speckled." As God assisted Jacob to work his plan using advanced animal husbandry, Laban's flocks - the ones with solid colors and not spotted and speckled - began to grow smaller and smaller. Jacob tried to assure Laban's family that he was simply arranging payment for his many years of faithful service to Laban, "And he said unto them, I see your father's countenance, that it is not toward me as before; but the God of my father hath been with me. And ye know that with all my power I have served your father. And your father hath deceived me, and changed my wages ten times; but God suffered him not to hurt me." (Genesis 31:5-7). His statement, "the God of my father hath been with me," was an understatement; the Lord was always with Jacob. Yet here, now, He made His Presence known by way of letting Jacob know he was strong enough to return to the Land of Canaan. He had sufficient possessions to co-exist with Esau, and he had sufficient men to defend Jacob's family from hurt at Esau's hands. God had provided just what Jacob needed to draw him

JACOB: A MAN OF DECEIT WHOM GOD LOVED

back to the Land of Promise, and that is where Jacob now intended to go.

It is good to assure ourselves of the fact that God is with us, and will provide all we need to face our enemies or the unknown.

Her Father's Images

"Then Jacob rose up, and set his sons and his wives upon camels; And he carried away all his cattle, and all his goods which he had gotten, the cattle of his getting, which he had gotten in Padan-aram, for to go to Isaac his father in the land of Canaan. And Laban went to shear his sheep: and Rachel had stolen the images that were her father's." Genesis 31:17-19

Jacob was duly concerned that Laban would strip him of all his prosperity, take back his daughters and grandsons, and possibly even kill Jacob. His mind strengthened by Rachel's declaration that what he had gained was nothing more than the dowry rightfully belonging to Leah and Rachel, Jacob decided to leave Laban's country and return to his father in Canaan. He was in the right on every point: He had faithfully served Laban according to his requirement, he had honestly gained the great wealth he now possessed, and - most important - he was following the Lord's leadership in returning to the Land of Promise. After all, Jacob was heir to the promises of God through the seed of Abraham. He was acting in response to God's reassurance concerning those promises. The fact that he stole away, so to speak, was merely practicing what is sometimes called "due diligence." He was not going to give Laban the opportunity to do him and his family harm. Laban did chase after Jacob, and eventually overtake and confront him at the border of the land of Canaan. He upbraided Jacob for leaving without giving Laban the opportunity to "throw him a going away party," but his concern was for possessions even dearer to him than the wealth Jacob had gained at his expense.

MEN OF LIKE PASSION

Rachel had stolen her father's little gods - the images he worshiped in his pagan religion. If you remember, Laban was great-nephew to Abraham who had followed God's call out of the land of Ur of the Chaldees, a land of idol worshipers. God delivered Abraham from idolatry, but apparently the rest of his family who left Ur as he did not leave their desire to serve idols. These little pieces of stone or metal meant a great deal to Laban. He chased Jacob for many miles for the main purpose of retrieving his idols. It also seems that the images meant a lot to Rachel. She apparently did not feel comfortable leaving her father's country without the images she had seen him worship. Here is the contrast, and it is worth our noting: Jacob served the Invisible God of all Creation - the God Who spoke to his fathers, Abraham and Isaac, and Who had spoken to him as well. He had never seen Him or His image. There is not doubt that Jacob had recounted all that God had told him to Rachel. After all, he loved her and a man wants to share his dreams and goals with the woman he loves. There also seems little doubt that Rachel wanted some insurance. She may have believed what Jacob told her of God's promises, but she was more comfortable with what she knew - what she could see - than merely to trust in an unseen hand guiding her husband. Does that sound familiar? God's people have always been warned to flee idolatry. It is an affront to our God. Rachel was willing to risk her life for the false assurance of keeping her father's images. If we serve "idols" today - that which we can see that we think gives us security - we are also risking our lives. Idolatry threatens our spiritual life and its privileges based on faith in God through His Son Jesus Christ.

It is good to bring our "little gods" out of their hiding place and fully trust in the Living God.

Rituals and Emblems

"Now therefore come thou, let us make a covenant, I and thou; and let it be for a witness between me and thee. And Jacob took a stone, and set it up for a pillar. And Jacob said unto his brethren, Gather stones; and they took stones, and made an heap: and they did eat there upon the heap." Genesis 31:44-46

After Laban overtook Jacob's fleeing tribe and searched for his little gods without success, Jacob took the opportunity to remind Laban of the whole situation's truth. Jacob had labored twenty years for Laban, who changed his wages "ten times," according to Jacob. This was simply a way of saying that Laban changed the terms of Jacob's service any time it appeared Jacob would gain the upper hand. Jacob's actions were simply to gain the wages Laban had promised, but had never delivered. Not only so, the Lord had appeared to Laban in a dream and warned him about bringing any harm to Jacob. Jacob emphasized this fact as something that was worthy of Laban's utmost attention, and Laban apparently agreed because he immediately solicited Jacob as an equal to enter into a covenant with him. This was no casual proposition. In those days men did not enter into covenants lightly, and even those who may not have wholly believed in the God of Abraham recognized the serious nature of entering into a vow where the name Jehovah was used as a seal of approval for the vow, or covenant. Laban's suggestion that he and Jacob enter into a covenant was so that they would have a record of their agreement to leave off making war one with the other. The ritual and emblems of the covenant were to remain as witnesses for all to see, and for future generations to be reminded that the two parties had agreed to be at peace with one another.

The ritual was solemn. The very word covenant meant that two parties walking between pieces of a sacrificed animal had established an agreement. They were in a sense "joined" by being between the pieces of the sacrifice. Jacob went farther by bringing in an emblem that had personal meaning to him. As he left the Land of Canaan over twenty years earlier and the Lord appeared to him in a dream, Jacob set up the stone he had used the previous night for a pillow as a pillar upon which to pour out a sacrifice drink offering. This is what he did now to establish the emblem of the covenant between Laban and him. He set up a stone for a pillar. This emblem was to serve as a memorial to the peace agreement - the covenant. It meant that both Jacob and Laban were promising never to pass by the pillar to pursue the other with intent to hurt or destroy. Jacob reinforced this by having his brethren gather stones to make a "heap," which Bible commentators say was a circle of stones upon which the men would have sat and eaten of the sacrifice together. Laban stated the true purpose of the covenant and its memorial when he said, "This heap is a witness between me and thee this day. Therefore was the name of it called Galeed; And Mizpah; for he said, The LORD watch between me and thee, when we are absent one from another" (Genesis 31:48-49). Laban "swore" by "the God of Abraham, and the God of Nahor, and the God of their father," even though he did not serve Abraham's God. He also equated the gods of Nahor and Abraham's father with Jehovah, but Jacob would not swear (affirm the covenant) by the gods of Mesopotamia; instead, he swore by the "fear of his father Isaac," showing his respect for the God of Abraham and Isaac. Once this ritual was over, Jacob entered into close communion with his brethren only. He "...offered sacrifice upon the mount, and called his brethren to eat bread: and they did eat bread, and tarried all night in the mount." Here is the lesson for us: rituals will not satisfy spiritual desires; only sacrifice and close communion with God and our brethren will do so.

It is good to offer our sacrifices of praise unto our God and seek close communion with other believers where possible. Interactions with unbelievers may be necessary but they are never spiritually satisfying.

God's Host

"And Jacob went on his way, and the angels of God met him. And when Jacob saw them, he said, This is God's host: and he called the name of that place Mahanaim. And Jacob sent messengers before him to Esau his brother unto the land of Seir, the country of Edom." Genesis 32:1-3

As he returned to the border of the Land of Canaan, Jacob camped at a place he called Mahanaim - meaning, "double camp." He called this place double camp because he perceived that God had encamped along side his camp, and he saw this as a confirmation that God was indeed with him. The sign of this confirmation was that the angels of God met him. Have you ever considered what it would be like to actually see the angels of God? They were there as messengers of the covenant God had made with Jacob over twenty years earlier. Jacob had seen the angels of God in a dream before, ascending and descending on a great ladder; but this passage does not say anything about a dream. Jacob not only saw the angels of God, the Bible says they "met him." Jacob did not just stumble across an encampment of God's angels. That is not the nature of angels. Many people seem to believe in angels today as beings with self-determination and powers to either aid or hinder people in their pursuits, as if they were independent agents of the supernatural. God's word is clear that angels do not operate independently; neither do they go about looking for "good" people to help with their problems. The Epistle to the Hebrews stated the sure truth of angels' purpose and actions. "Are they not all ministering spirits, sent forth to minister for them who shall be heirs of salvation?" (Hebrews 1:14). The heirs of salvation are the only recipients of the ministry of God's host of angels. Their ministry is not to assist with gaining health, wealth, or any other natural advantage. They minister the hope of Christ to God's people.

As the angels of God met Jacob, he immediately recognized their source and their purpose. "This is God's host," he said. How awe inspiring it is to realize that the host of God had been dispatched to minister for this one heir of salvation! How equally awesome it is to realize that the same host of God is dispatched to minister unto each one of God's little children still today. The angels' purpose was to confirm God's Presence with Jacob - in keeping with the promise He had made Jacob twenty years earlier. "And, behold, I am with thee, and will keep thee in all places whither thou goest, and will bring thee again into this land; for I will not leave thee, until I have done that which I have spoken to thee of" (Genesis 28:15). God had been with Jacob throughout his years of labor with Laban, and he was with him as he neared the land of his father, Isaac. Was this it? Was Jacob now on his own? No, the strength of the promise of God's Presence with Jacob (and us) was, "...I will not leave thee, until I have done that which I have spoken to thee of." God was not going to leave Jacob nor suffer harm to come to him because Christ was in him - the promise of the Seed of Abraham was yet to be fulfilled through the line of Jacob. The same promise is still true for us today, because of what Paul called, "Christ in you, the hope of glory." God is not through with us yet. He has promised eternal, heavenly, sinless existence for each one for whom Christ died. In that sense, we dwell in Mahanaim daily, the place of "two camps." God is with us and will keep us until the day He fulfills His promises in Christ. That is the assurance Jacob received as the angels of God met him, and that is our assurance as well.

It is good to realize that, "The angel of the LORD encampeth round about them that fear him, and delivereth them" (Psalm 34:7).

Jacob's Humility

"And Jacob said, O God of my father Abraham, and God of my father Isaac, the LORD which saidst unto me, Return unto thy country, and to thy kindred, and I will deal well with thee: I am not worthy of the least of all the mercies, and of all the truth, which thou hast showed unto thy servant; for with my staff I passed over this Jordan; and now I am become two bands. Deliver me, I pray thee, from the hand of my brother, from the hand of Esau: for I fear him, lest he will come and smite me, and the mother with the children. And thou saidst, I will surely do thee good, and make thy seed as the sand of the sea, which

JACOB: A MAN OF DECEIT WHOM GOD LOVED

cannot be numbered for multitude." Genesis 32:9-12

Even though the Lord had assured Jacob of His divine Presence by sending His angels to meet him as Jacob came near the Land of Canaan, he felt he had some cause for concern. His brother Esau had threatened to kill him over twenty years before for supplanting Esau in receiving the blessing of the first born son from their father Isaac. Jacob had purchased the birthright, or rights of the firstborn son, from Esau - whom the Bible says "despised" it; but still the father's blessing would have gone to Esau had Jacob not deceived Isaac into thinking he was blessing Esau while he was actually blessing Jacob. True, twenty years had passed since that time of deception; but Jacob had no reason to think that Esau had changed his mind. Now, as he came near to the land in which Esau dwelt, Jacob sent his messengers to Esau to let him know he was returning and that the Lord had prospered him for his two decades of labor for their Uncle Laban. He told the men to tell Esau, "...I have oxen, and asses, flocks, and menservants, and women servants: and I have sent to tell my lord, that I may find grace in thy sight." He was not bragging about his wealth. Instead, Jacob was showing humility in his return to his brother Esau. He not only showed Esau that he did not need the possessions he would have inherited as the recipient of Isaac's blessing, but he also showed that he did not consider himself to be worthy of the rights of the firstborn son. Jacob, as the holder of the firstborn son's preeminence, had every right to receive honor and respect from Esau; yet, Jacob in his message to Esau called him, "my lord." When his messengers returned from having delivered his peace missive to Esau, they told Jacob that Esau was coming to meet him with 400 men. Jacob feared for his and his family's safety, so he took appropriate steps.

He first prepared naturally by dividing his family into two camps so that if Esau destroyed one "company," the other could escape. Then Jacob prepared spiritually. His prayer to God was an humble prayer of supplication. We might wonder here if such a prayer showed a lack of faith on Jacob's part. Not at all! But, had the Lord not reassured

Jacob that He was with him when He sent His angels? Yes, that was a wonderful assurance; but this was an immediate need that Jacob felt deeply and that could only be met by the Lord. This was not a lack of faith; in fact, Jacob's prayer was a definite display of humble trust in the preserving power of God's grace and mercy. If you feel yourself to be a child of God, you know that your sins have been forgiven. Why, then, do you cry out when you feel the weight of sin upon you from time to time for the Lord to forgive your sins? God's word tells us that If we confess our sins, he is faithful and just to forgive us our sins and to cleanse us from all unrighteousness. We are not showing a lack of faith when we pray for daily cleansing; we are showing the depth of our faith. Jacob's prayer showed his humility toward God. "I am not worthy of the least of all the mercies, and of all the truth, which thou hast showed unto thy servant;" God would honor Jacob's humility and answer his humble prayer. So will He answer our prayers when we humbly call upon Him.

It is good to pray as did the lowly Publican in one of Jesus' parables, "Lord, be merciful to me, a sinner."

A Prince, With God

"And Jacob called the name of the place Peniel: for I have seen God face to face, and my life is preserved. And as he passed over Penuel the sun rose upon him, and he halted upon his thigh. Therefore the children of Israel eat not of the sinew which shrank, which is upon the hollow of the thigh, unto this day: because he touched the hollow of Jacob's thigh in the sinew that shrank." Genesis 32:30-32

Having heard from the messengers he sent to Esau that he was on his way with what Jacob thought was an army of 400 men to possibly do him harm, Jacob sprang into action. Not only did he pray, but he also devised a plan whereby he would continue to try to appease the wrath of Esau. He selected a good number of cattle from among his

JACOB: A MAN OF DECEIT WHOM GOD LOVED

herd and divided them into four separate divisions. This was to send to meet Esau with gifts as he approached Jacob and his family. The very way that Jacob chose to send these gifts showed his nature: he never gave up. From the time of his birth, Jacob depended on his own strength and determination to get what he thought was rightfully his. Called the "heel catcher," Jacob the second born had grabbed the heel of Esau the firstborn to use him to pull him out of their mother's womb into the light of day. He had used his wit and guile to supplant Esau and gain the blessing of the firstborn son. He had labored twenty years to gain the wife he wanted and to gain wealth at Laban's expense. Now, he was again using all his faculties of self-dependence to ensure his safe return to the land of his father Isaac. Esau was an obstacle that stood in his way. Yes, he was sending Esau gifts; but he was doing so to remove the obstacle. It is true that he feared for the safety of his family as well, and that is what caused his actions to try to maintain the upper hand. Jacob the "Heel Catcher,' the Supplanter, was about to be given another name - one that resulted in his being shown his need to rely on God's strength more than his own.

He took his wives, maidservants, and children and went away from the main party toward a brook of water at a fording place called Jabbock. After depositing them on the safe side of the brook, Jacob crossed back over to await his brother Esau; but God had another visitor in mind for Jacob - one who would enter into a battle of wills with Jacob and emerge victorious, with Jacob clinging to him for strength. Jacob met a "man" there at the ford of Jabbock who "wrestled" with him "until the breaking of the day." Jacob, true to his nature, would not give in to the man who wrestled him, so the "man," with supernatural powers, touched the hollow of Jacob's thigh to cause it to go out of joint. The one critical place of strength and leverage that allows a man to wrestle and gain strength over an opponent is the joint between his hip and thigh. If that place is without strength, the man cannot even stand on his own. That is exactly the lesson God's "man" was there to teach Jacob: You cannot stand on your own,

MEN OF LIKE PASSION

Jacob. You've prevailed up to now through your wit and strength of will, using your guile and stubbornness as tools of strength by which you think you have prevailed. This was the message the "man" of God was sent to teach Jacob. Even now, however, with no strength of his own with which to stand, Jacob clung to the man he wrestled with. Finally, the man said, "Let me go, for the day breaketh." Jacob refused to let go of him until the man "blessed" him. Does this sound familiar? The messenger of God had come to bless Jacob, and he would do so; but he wanted Jacob to understand that this blessing came from his standing - his place - with God (as it were, clinging to Him for strength) and not from Jacob's own strength. He asked Jacob his name. "Supplanter," said Jacob as he told him his given name. The name by which we know Jacob's family and the nation that sprang from him from that point forward was given him by the man who said, "Thy name shall be called no more Jacob, but Israel: for as a prince hast thou power with God and with men, and hast prevailed." Relying on his own strength, Jacob was known as the Supplanter; when he relied on God's strength, he became known as Israel, meaning "A prince with God." He would rule when he relied on God's strength. He would serve when he relied on his own. So it is with God's children today. We can "rule" over our fleshly nature when we rely on God's strength. We serve our fleshly nature when we rely on our own strength.

Today is a perfect day to rule as a prince, with God.

Family Reunion

"And Jacob lifted up his eyes, and looked, and, behold, Esau came, and with him four hundred men. And he divided the children unto Leah, and unto Rachel, and unto the two handmaids. And he put the handmaids and their children foremost, and Leah and her children after, and Rachel and Joseph hindermost. And he passed over before them, and bowed himself to the ground seven times, until he came

JACOB: A MAN OF DECEIT WHOM GOD LOVED

near to his brother. And Esau ran to meet him, and embraced him, and fell on his neck, and kissed him: and they wept." Genesis 33:1-4

Jacob's worst fear seemed to be looming on the horizon. Esau and his 400 men were within sight and must have presented a fearsome picture to Jacob. He sprang into action, separating his little family into "waves" as they waited for Esau's company to meet them. The order of each wave seems to be significant. First were the handmaids and their children, then Leah and her children, and finally Rachel and her son Joseph. If Esau's intent was to destroy Jacob and his family, Jacob obviously wanted to give the source of his first love and his heir by her to have the greatest chance of surviving. Rather than hold this up to today's standards we think to be fair, let's try to apply it and get a lesson from it. If you had to prioritize parts of your life to give up today, what part would you give up first? What part would try to make every effort to preserve? You would put that part about which you cared the most last in line to give up, wouldn't you? If we applied this to our family, jobs, recreation, and service to the Lord, how would you line them up? Where would your first love be? The good thing about Jacob's case is that he did not need to do this. Esau meant him no harm.

As Esau approached, Jacob went in front of his family and humbled himself before Esau seven times. Jacob was not trying to show how strong he was, he was showing his perfect humility and willingness to recognize Esau's position. Much to his surprise, Esau also showed humility in running to meet Jacob. He embraced Jacob, not in a half-hearted way, but by falling on his neck. This showed he was genuinely moved at the sight of his brother. Both brothers wept. This was not common in those days. Grown men did not display this kind of emotion as a rule. Family disagreements are terrible. They cause people who ought to love one another and want to be with one another to remain separated for much too long, sometimes. Both men had matured, obviously. As they went through the custom of Jacob offering Esau gifts and Esau declining, each man then showed he needed nothing from the other. They were not threat to each other - at least not at that moment. Their heirs would prove that this peace did not last; but, for the moment, Jacob and Esau were reunited as natural brethren. In this, God had showed Jacob that He was preserving his life and his children's lives. Esau had become a great nation naturally, but Israel's inheritance was that he would become a great nation spiritually.

It is good to meditate on where our first love lies in our priorities.

Go Up to Bethel

"And God said unto Jacob, Arise, go up to Bethel, and dwell there: and make there an altar unto God, that appeared unto thee when thou fleddest from the face of Esau thy brother. Then Jacob said unto his household, and to all that were with him, Put away the strange gods that are among you, and be clean, and change your garments: And let us arise, and go up to Bethel; and I will make there an altar unto God, who answered me in the day of my distress, and was with me in the way which I went." Genesis 35:1-3

Much had happened since Jacob and his family had entered back into the land of Canaan. Delivered from any threat from Esau, Jacob had traveled to a place called Shechem where he purchased a parcel of land and pitched his tents. He probably would have dwelt there happily for the rest of his life if trouble had not arisen. He was in the midst of people who did not follow the same God he followed, nor did they live by the same moral code. Even though Jacob had two wives and two concubines, this was in keeping with the moral code of his day, even if it was not in keeping with God's law of one woman for one man. Before we condemn Jacob for his situation, we should remember that God had chosen Jacob to be the head of a great family, and He continued to bless Jacob and lead him throughout his life.

JACOB: A MAN OF DECEIT WHOM GOD LOVED

The trouble that arose had to do with his and Leah's daughter, Dinah. Shechem, a young man of that country and the one for whom the place would be later named, saw Dinah as she left the safety of her father's encampment and went to "see how the other half lived." If we think about this, we might agree that such behavior is still the cause of a great deal of trouble for God's people. We are curious about how others live who are not called of God to be a separate people, as we are. Rather than praise God for His mercy in calling us away from the normal concern for gaining possessions in this world, we sometimes want to see how unbelievers are doing. That is essentially what Dinah did. The problem was that, "when Shechem the son of Hamor the Hivite, prince of the country, saw her, he took her, and lay with her, and defiled her." There are many spiritual lessons we could draw from this, but it gets worse. Jacob's sons devised an intricate scheme to get revenge on Shechem and his kinsman, even though Shechem expressed a desire to "do the right thing." He wanted Jacob to give him Leah's hand in marriage, and his father strongly encouraged Jacob and his family to become full-fledged members of the community by taking wives of the daughters of that land and giving its inhabitants their daughters. Doesn't that sound reasonable, from a natural standpoint? After all, shouldn't God's people try to get along with others who do not believe in His ways, who serve other gods?

Dinah's brothers, Simeon and Levi the sons of Leah, took advantage of their brothers' scheme - that of tricking Shechem, his father, and all the men of that city to submit themselves to being circumcised. To further their thirst for revenge, they used a precious emblem of God's covenant with the seed of Abraham to fool the men into thinking that submitting themselves to that act would make them acceptable as future husbands for the women of Jacob's family. All along the sons of Jacob meant to use circumcision to weaken the men of Shechem's strength so they could gain the upper hand; and that is exactly what happened. Simeon and Levi killed the inhabitants of Shechem, stole their cattle and possessions, spoiled their city, and took captive their wives and children. They went far beyond the normal scope of acts of revenge. Whether we look at it as an outgrowth of their rage or as a manifestation of their nature, the acts they committed were atrocious, unforgivable, and seemed far worse than Shechem's act that supposedly caused their extreme actions. The reaction by Jacob was one of disgust and fear. His sons had committed ungodly acts and soiled his name. Worse, they gave occasion for unbelievers to blaspheme their God. Jacob knew he must leave that area and take his family with him to preserve their lives. It was at this point that God reminded Jacob of a place he had not seen for well over twenty years: Bethel. That certain place Jacob had seen the angels of God ascending and descending on a ladder set up between earth and heaven was the exact spot the Lord told Jacob to go to. God was leading Jacob back to that spot physically, but He was also leading him back spiritually. Jacob knew that his family had adopted the ways of the people around them to the point that they were keeping "little gods," idols, which they no doubt had put some stock in. Jacob's directions to his family were to put away the idols, clean themselves up, and put on garments worthy of the sacred place called Bethel. Good advice for them, and good advice for us still today. God's people need to arise and go up to Bethel spiritually. It is high time for us to get back to that separated place where we can worship and serve God acceptably.

It is good to arise and go to Bethel.

God Almighty Blesses Israel

"And God appeared unto Jacob again, when he came out of Padan-aram, and blessed him. And God said unto him, Thy name is Jacob: thy name shall not be called any more Jacob, but Israel shall be thy name: and he called his name Israel. And God said unto him, I am God Almighty: be fruitful and multiply; a nation and a company of nations shall be of thee, and kings shall come out of thy loins; And the

JACOB: A MAN OF DECEIT WHOM GOD LOVED

land which I gave Abraham and Isaac, to thee I will give it, and to thy seed after thee will I give the land." Genesis 35:9-12

Jacob had returned to Bethel, the place where the Lord had appeared to him so many years before. He returned in haste, fearful that the inhabitants of Canaan would pursue his family and do them all harm. It was at Bethel, however, that the Lord reinforced the promises He had made there to Jacob over twenty years earlier. He revealed His great Name to Jacob, gave Jacob a new name by which he and his descendants would be known forever, and reaffirmed the promises of Abraham and Isaac with Jacob. First, the Lord reaffirmed Jacob's new name - Israel, the one the angel of the Lord had given Jacob as he wrestled with him at the brook Jabbock. The name meant, "he will rule as God," or "God prevails," or "a prince with God." Each of these meanings denotes the standing with God that Jacob's new name would come to represent, not only with him personally but also with his twelve sons and their posterity. One central characteristic of mankind is every man's desire to "make a name" for himself. Jacob had been willing to supplant Esau's natural right to the position of prince of Isaac's family and deceive his father into granting him the blessing that position was entitled to. He wanted to make himself a name, he wanted to be the prince, he wanted to "rule" over the other members of his family. His was a natural desire, but God has a better way than any natural system can afford. God made a name for Jacob, He declared him to be a prince, and He appointed him to rule over "...a nation and a company of nations...and kings shall come out of thy loins" His family of twelve sons would become twelve tribes, then a great nation. Finally, a company of nations would come under the influence of God's dealings with Jacob - now called Israel - and great kings would reign over his posterity

Not only did God give Jacob a new name, but He also revealed His own name to Jacob in a new way. "And God said unto him, I am God Almighty." El Shaddai, God Almighty, revealed Himself to Israel and reaffirmed the promises He had made to his grandfather Abraham, his father Isaac, and earlier to Jacob: "And the land which I gave Abraham and Isaac, to thee I will give it, and to thy seed after thee will I give the land." Here is an ironic point: El Shaddai stated that He gave the land to Abraham and to Isaac. They never owned more than a few square feet Abraham purchased for a burying spot. In fact, the New Testament's Epistle to the Hebrews says of the three of them, "By faith he" (Abraham) "sojourned in the land of promise, as in a strange country, dwelling in tabernacles with Isaac and Jacob, the heirs with him of the same promise" (Hebrews 11:9). God Almighty's promises to Israel were by the promise of inheritance. Jacob had sought it by deceit through natural means, but God meant him to have it by the truth of His word through spiritual means. So it is with our eternal inheritance: we cannot obtain it or attain to it by natural means; we can only do so by the grace of God through the spiritual means He provides. Jesus, natural heir of Jacob in the flesh, said of His heavenly Father, "God is a Spirit: and they that worship him must worship him in spirit and in truth" (John 4:24). The only way the old supplanter and deceiver formerly known as Jacob could inherit the spiritual promises of God Almighty was that He called Jacob by a new name, declared his inheritance, and directed his path to receive it and walk in it. God Almighty also calls us by a new name, declares us to be joint heirs with His Son, Jesus Christ, and directs our path to receive and walk in that inheritance.

It is good to follow the path in which God leads us, to enjoy our inheritance.

Life Comes from Death

"And they journeyed from Bethel; and there was but a little way to come to Ephrath: and Rachel travailed, and she had hard labor. And it came to pass, when she was in hard labor, that the midwife said unto her, Fear not; thou shalt have this son also. And it came to pass,

JACOB: A MAN OF DECEIT WHOM GOD LOVED

as her soul was in departing, (for she died) that she called his name Ben-oni: but his father called him Benjamin. And Rachel died, and was buried in the way to Ephrath, which is Bethlehem. And Jacob set a pillar upon her grave: that is the pillar of Rachel's grave unto this day." Genesis 35:16-20

Having been blessed by God Almighty at Bethel, Jacob and his family began to make their way from Bethel southward to Hebron, where Isaac dwelt. It was probably a slow moving caravan, because Rachel was once again expecting a child. Up until now, Joseph was her only heir; so another child would be a great blessing to Rachel. Sadly, she would not live to see the child grow up. As they neared a place called Ephrath, the time came that Rachel should be delivered and her labor was very hard. It became apparent to the attending midwife that Rachel might not survive the ordeal, but she wanted to encourage Rachel in her delivery. "Fear not; thou shalt have this son also," the midwife told her. She was letting Rachel know that she was giving Jacob another son. In fact, he would be the twelfth son of Jacob, beloved brother to Joseph, and last of the heads of the twelve tribes that comprised the nation soon to be called Israel; but Rachel would not see any of this. She gave the baby a name, however, and as the custom was then, his name would be associated with the conditions of his birth. She called his name Ben-oni, which means "son of my sorrow." Her earthly life was at an end and she would never get to see the baby grow and prosper, so it is completely understandable that Rachel would give him such a name. The wondrous part of this story is that, in Rachel's passing, we are given a deep reassurance of life continuing after our earthly existence.

It was "as her soul was in departing" that she named the baby Ben-oni. Her sorrow was of an earthly sort, but the fact that her soul departed shows us that her joy was ready to become full. David, an heir of the great nation that would come from the twelve tribes of Israel, would later say of the experience of passing from life on earth to the realm of eternal life, "In thy presence is fulness of joy." In the presence of the hard labor, and of the birth of a son she would never get to rejoice in on earth, Rachel had great sorrow. Hence, the name Ben-Oni; but her sorrow was about to turn to pure joy as her soul left her mortal body and entered into the Presence of the Lord. There is an old hymn sung in the early days of this country - and still in some Old Baptist hymnals - with a verse that reads in part, "Why do we mourn departing friends and shake at death's alarm? 'Tis but the voice that Jesus sends to call them to His arms." Rachel's sorrow was over, and her joy was just beginning; but Jacob and his family were left to mourn her passing. He buried her there, near to present day Bethlehem, and set a pillar upon her grave. This was not merely a grave marker. To "set a pillar" meant that Jacob very likely set up an altar there and offered sacrifices unto God in thankfulness for the memory of his first love. Not willing to have his youngest son bear the name that would memorialize the sorrow of her passing, Jacob called the baby Benjamin, or son of my right hand. The name also meant, "son that is particularly dear to me." Jacob would rather memorialize the joy that Rachel had brought to him, and the blessed state in which he believed her departed soul to be rejoicing, rather than to memorialize the sorrow of her passing. What great hope this ought to give us that one day our soul shall also depart - if the Lord tarries His coming - to a blessed state of fullness of joy.

It is good to remember that our earthly existence, as full of sorrow as it may be, is not the end. Joy awaits us. Life will come from death.

Jacob Dwelt In The Land

"And Jacob dwelt in the land wherein his father was a stranger, in the land of Canaan." Genesis 37:1

This seems a simple statement about the place where Jacob dwelt, but it contains much to show us the character of this man whom

JACOB: A MAN OF DECEIT WHOM GOD LOVED

God had chosen to further the cause of Christ. God's word tells us that Isaac died and was buried by his sons, Esau and Jacob. Then, for some strange reason, the Holy Spirit inspires Moses to record in a whole chapter of the Book of Genesis the lineage of Esau. Every son and every grandson, at least, have their names recorded. Not only that, but we are also told that Esau and his heirs left the land of Canaan and went into the country, meaning outside what would later be called the Promised Land, and so, "Thus dwelt Esau in mount Seir: Esau is Edom." The Edomites would later plague the Children of Israel mercilessly, but this passing from each other seems rather peaceable. After all, both Jacob and Esau were now rich men. So great were their possessions in fact, that the Bible says, "For their riches were more than that they might dwell together; and the land wherein they were strangers could not bear them because of their cattle." Please note this little, obscure fact: in Canaan, they were strangers. As rich as they were, they had no land upon which they could freely graze their vast holdings of cattle. Their wealth of possessions actually hindered them in the land wherein they walked as strangers, and they had to depend on the permission of others to stay. As was typical of his character, Esau abandoned the land, "wherein his father was a stranger," the land God had promised the seed of Abraham, and went to make his own way; but Jacob stayed.

His staying in the land of Canaan, the land wherein his father was a stranger, was an act of faith. God had spoken to Jacob more than once and assured him that He would give him the land. It might have been easier for Jacob to do as Esau did, and strike out on his own to conquer other lands and take them for his own. He probably was strong enough that he could have raised an army of his heirs and servants and taken a portion of the land of Canaan by force; but God did not promise Jacob a portion of the land: He promised him all of it. If we abandon the natural side of this promise for a moment and dwell on the spiritual side, perhaps we can draw a parallel to the religious age in which we live. Many people today are being told that there is a formula by which they, as believers in God, may have abundant natural blessings: health, wealth, happiness, positions of power, and so forth. They are told that their obtaining these things is predicated on their being strong enough in faith to "take" these things (some say name it and claim it.) There is nothing wrong with a believer in Jesus Christ being in possession of health, wealth, happiness, or power; but to spend spiritual currency pursuing these things is to desire only a portion of the blessings. It is akin to taking - by force - only a portion of the Land of Promise. That is where the simple statement of Jacob's existence ought to bring us back to the place of seeing that God has more, much more, for His people than just material blessings. Jacob dwelt in the land wherein his father was a stranger. This heir to the great promises of Abraham chose to follow God's leadership and God's timetable for accomplishing His will, and so he truly became heir to the blessings Abraham possessed - spiritual and not natural. Jacob is mentioned as a man of faith in the same manner of Abraham in Hebrews 11:9-10, "By faith he sojourned in the land of promise, as in a strange country, dwelling in tabernacles with Isaac and Jacob, the heirs with him of the same promise: For he looked for a city which hath foundations, whose builder and maker is God." Jacob was an heir with Abraham of the same promise: a safe and sure dwelling place that God would provide for them.

It is good to remember, and reaffirm, that we are walking and dwelling in a natural land wherein our fathers were strangers, but as heirs with them of the promise of a greater spiritual land that God has prepared for us.

Jacob Rose Up

"And Jacob rose up from Beer-sheba: and the sons of Israel carried Jacob their father, and their little ones, and their wives, in the wagons which Pharaoh had sent to carry him. And they took their cattle, and

JACOB: A MAN OF DECEIT WHOM GOD LOVED

their goods, which they had gotten in the land of Canaan, and came into Egypt, Jacob, and all his seed with him:" Genesis 46:5-6

Much had happened to Jacob as he left what had been the dwelling place of his father Isaac at Beer-sheba. His sons had sold their brother Joseph into bondage, and Joseph had ultimately prospered in Egypt. A great famine took hold of that part of the world, most especially in the land of Canaan, and caused Jacob to send his sons to Egypt to buy grain. What then took place is what the world calls irony, but what God calls the counsel of His own will. Jacob's ten oldest sons went to Egypt to buy grain from the man they had heard the Pharaoh had placed in charge of all his goods. After a time, Joseph revealed himself to them as the brother they had left for dead and then sold into slavery many years earlier. He wanted to see his father and younger brother Benjamin, but Joseph was acting according to God's good counsel when he sent wagons with his brothers to fetch his father and the whole family and bring them down into Egypt where he knew he could provide for them. Famine would not claim Jacob's family; in fact, they were given a place where they and their flocks would grow and prosper. Jacob did not fear going to Egypt. In one sense, he was following the pattern set by his grandfather Abraham and his father Isaac, because they had also gone to Egypt when famine threatened their family; but Jacob's family would stay for hundreds of years before they finally returned. Jacob had God's promise that their return would not be as a small family, but in a far greater capacity.

Jacob had come to Beer-sheba to offer sacrifices unto the God of his father Isaac. As he did so, the Lord spoke to Jacob - in visions of the night - and once again assured Jacob of His Presence and favor. God said, "I am God, the God of thy father: fear not to go down into Egypt; for I will there make of thee a great nation: I will go down with thee into Egypt; and I will also surely bring thee up again: and Joseph shall put his hand upon thine eyes." While it is true that Jacob would never see the land of Canaan again, it is also true that

Israel, the great nation that God promised to make of Jacob's little band, would one day leave Egypt with a strong arm. God would make good on His promises to Jacob: He was with Israel all the days they were in Egypt, He prepared and established a deliverer of His people in Jacob's descendant Moses, and He showed His power over all the powers of Egypt when He delivered His people from bondage. Would Jacob die in Egypt? Yes, but even in that God promised him great things. He would see Joseph his son again, and Joseph would be there to "put his hand" upon the eyes of Jacob as they closed in death. God's natural promises to Jacob were to be realized in Israel, and His spiritual promises were to be realized in Christ. When the Lord said to Jacob, "fear not to go down into Egypt," Jacob heard and obeyed. Why should we fear the future, when God has promised us eternal inheritance with Him? Fear not!

It is good to establish ourselves once again on the surety of God's promises.

Jacob Blessed Pharaoh

"And Joseph brought in Jacob his father, and set him before Pharaoh: and Jacob blessed Pharaoh. And Pharaoh said unto Jacob, How old art thou? And Jacob said unto Pharaoh, The days of the years of my pilgrimage are an hundred and thirty years: few and evil have the days of the years of my life been, and have not attained unto the days of the years of the life of my fathers in the days of their pilgrimage." Genesis 47:7-9

After he had safely guided his father's family into the land of Goshen, Joseph took his father to present him to Pharaoh. This was a common courtesy for a man visiting in another country, and no doubt was attended with much pomp and circumstance. After all, here was a lowly shepherd from a poor country, probably having nothing to bring before the Pharaoh as a gift, being presented to a head

JACOB: A MAN OF DECEIT WHOM GOD LOVED

of state - a king! Joseph was fulfilling the social requirements of the day, perhaps; but Jacob came before Pharaoh as one convinced that he was blessed of God. He understood this was a far greater honor than any thing he could receive at the hand of this king - who in the final analysis was just a man like Jacob. He had the power that his kingdom afforded him, but Pharaoh served at the pleasure of God Almighty. In fact, Paul tells us that the Lord, "raised up Pharaoh" to accomplish His purpose in him. How often do God's people become overwhelmed with the thought of being in the presence of some person the world counts as great, or powerful, or influential? The God we serve is much greater than any power or influence in the world! In fact, He tells us in His word that He raises up kings and kingdoms and He puts them down. Jacob had a good perspective on the situation.

There is no doubt that Jacob was respectful of Pharaoh's position. He understood himself to be a guest in Egypt - just as he was a stranger in the land of Canaan. What's more, Jacob fully understood and believed that his people's stay in Egypt was a temporary one. They were blessed of God, and He had something better for them. The land of Goshen was a good and fertile land, and Israel would prosper there; but Goshen was not the Land of Promise. Jacob appreciated the blessings that Goshen represented to his family, but he did not attribute those blessings to Pharaoh; instead, he gave all praise and glory to God for preserving him and his family. As he stood before Pharaoh, as God's ambassador, Jacob did something that seems insignificant, but that shows the mighty power of God working in his life. Jacob blessed Pharaoh. We could miss this little statement if not careful. In the sense of blessings, the person bestowing the blessing is understood to be the one in a power position, and the one receiving the blessing is understood to be the one in a "need" position. In fact, Paul's Letter to the Hebrews tells us, "And without all contradiction the less is blessed of the better." What a wondrous show of God's might and power in the life of a man for whom the world would have

MEN OF LIKE PASSION

little esteem. Jacob, in blessing Pharaoh, showed his primary hope was in the Eternal Provider of all good things.

It is good to refresh our hope in the provision of God's blessings, and not in what the world can provide to us.

Jacob's End

"And his sons did unto him according as he commanded them: For his sons carried him into the land of Canaan, and buried him in the cave of the field of Machpelah, which Abraham bought with the field for a possession of a burial place of Ephron the Hittite, before Mamre." Genesis 50:12-13

Jacob lived seventeen years in Egypt and died at the ripe old age of 147. Before he died, he gave his family a token of the faith he still had in God's promises. Jacob made Joseph swear that he would honor his wishes to be buried in the Land of Canaan, "bury me not, I pray thee, in Egypt: But I will lie with my fathers, and thou shalt carry me out of Egypt, and bury me in their burial place" (Genesis 47:29-30). Even though he now could have no hope of inheriting the natural land of Canaan, Jacob showed that his hope was in God; and God had made promises to him that were not dependent on him, but on his seed. There was a cave in the field of Machpelah on the plains of Mamre near Hebron that held those that were heirs with him of the same promises. Abraham and Isaac were buried there. Abraham, Jacob's grandfather, had purchased this spot for a burial place and it was the only spot that either he or Isaac, Jacob's father, had ever owned in the land God promised them. Jacob had purchased a portion of land next to this many years before he and his family went down into Egypt, and that was the place of his hope. It was a token of hope to the children of Israel as they dwelt in Egypt for over four hundred years. Jacob's end may seem of little consequence - a man who lived and died, never having received the end of his faith concerning the

JACOB: A MAN OF DECEIT WHOM GOD LOVED

natural promises of God; but his passing was a testimony of the faith in God Almighty that characterized his life, and it bears a closer look.

A little less than four hundred years after his passing, Jacob's family had become a great nation in terms of their numbers and God delivered them out of Egypt to make good on the promise He had first made to Abraham. As this nation of tribes traveled toward Canaan, the king of Moab hired an eastern seer named Balaam to come and place a curse upon them. God would not allow him to do so; in fact, He caused Balaam to pronounce blessings upon His people. These blessings were couched in reference to Jacob. Balaam stated in one blessing, "Who can count the dust of Jacob, and the number of the fourth part of Israel? Let me die the death of the righteous, and let my last end be like his!" (Numbers 23:10). The testimony of Jacob's life was captured in the end of his life: he died the death of the righteous. He died in faith, just as he had lived in faith. Balaam further said of Jacob, "How goodly are thy tents, O Jacob, and thy tabernacles, O Israel! As the valleys are they spread forth, as gardens by the river's side, as the trees of lign aloes which the LORD hath planted, and as cedar trees beside the waters. He shall pour the water out of his buckets, and his seed shall be in many waters, and his king shall be higher than Agag, and his kingdom shall be exalted. God brought him forth out of Egypt; he hath as it were the strength of a unicorn: he shall eat up the nations his enemies, and shall break their bones, and pierce them through with his arrows. He couched, he lay down as a lion, and as a great lion: who shall stir him up? Blessed is he that blesseth thee, and cursed is he that curseth thee" (Numbers 24:5-9). Balaam saw that God had blessed Jacob naturally and spiritually, and as he looked upon Israel encamped there on the plains of Moab, he prophesied of the blessings yet to come for God's people. That is what Jacob saw by faith, and that is how he lived his life after God revealed His Presence as a guiding force in Jacob's life. We would do well to model ourselves after Jacob, to believe in God's blessings still to

◄ **MEN OF LIKE PASSION**

come and to live with the knowledge that He is with us. Then our end may be as Jacob's: we can die in faith as we have lived in faith.

It is good to set our sights on God's promises and model our lives on the hope of Christ, just as Jacob did.

Joseph: A Man for Whom God Meant Good

Coat of Many Colors

"Now Israel loved Joseph more than all his children, because he was the son of his old age: and he made him a coat of many colors. And when his brethren saw that their father loved him more than all his brethren, they hated him, and could not speak peaceably unto him." Genesis 37:3-4

Most people are aware of the story of Joseph's coat of many colors; but they may not know what that coat represented. Jacob, son of Isaac and grandson of Abraham, was an old man when his eleventh son was born. Joseph was the firstborn son of Rachel, Jacob's beloved wife. She had been barren for a long time, so Joseph was looked on as a great blessing to Jacob; and he doted on Joseph. His other children were fully grown and Jacob - called Israel by the Lord - treated Joseph as a special son. In fact, Joseph was a very special son. He was obedient to his father and treated him with great respect. He honored the fact that Jacob - Israel - had been chosen by the Lord to continue to promises given to Abraham. When his brothers' behavior dishonored Jacob's standing in the land wherein they all dwelt, Joseph let his father know about it. In turn, Jacob honored Joseph. He did so not only because he was the son of his old age, but also because Joseph held the same values and love of God's promises as did his father. The coat

MEN OF LIKE PASSION

of many colors that Jacob made Joseph was a token of Jacob's love for Joseph, but it became the symbol of the hatred his brother's jealousy generated in them toward Joseph.

Bright colored clothing was not commonplace in that time; the coat would have caused Joseph to stand out and was a constant reminder to his brothers of the preference their father had for Joseph. It was also a symbol of the spiritual excellence of Joseph. Here is the question for us: why did Joseph's brethren hate him? Was it just because they desired more of their father's favor? No, they probably saw Joseph as a potential threat to their own inheritance. If they desired to be closer to their father and more well thought of they could have achieved this by honoring him and his relationship with the Lord. They did not desire this. Their nature was to hate the spiritual excellence in Joseph that the coat was merely a symbol of. Why does the world hate a sincere follower of Jesus Christ? It is easy to say that they do so because they do not love the Lord. It is more likely that they hate the moral excellence and condemnation of sin that the sincere follower of Jesus represents. The righteousness of Christ as shown by the sincere believer is like the coat of many colors - it stands out, and it points out the excellence of Christ. Joseph's brothers hated him because the coat of many colors pointed out his excellence and their shortcomings. The world at large hates sincere followers of Christ for the same reason. Just as Joseph's brethren did not love the promise of Christ as received through God's promises to Abraham, neither do unbelievers today love the promises of Christ. Even though Joseph's brethren hated him and his coat, Joseph wore it to honor his father. What about you? Are you wearing your "coat of many colors" - the righteousness of Christ - to honor your heavenly Father?

I pray that we may stand out today!

Dreamed A Dream

"And Joseph dreamed a dream, and he told it his brethren: and they hated him yet the more. And he said unto them, Hear, I pray you, this dream which I have dreamed: For, behold, we were binding sheaves in the field, and, lo, my sheaf arose, and also stood upright; and, behold, your sheaves stood round about, and made obeisance to my sheaf." Genesis 37:5-7

There was absolutely no natural reason for Joseph to tell his brothers his dream, at least not if he expected them to react reasonably to it. In his dream, they bowed down to him, as family members would do to the prince of the family. This honor was normally reserved for the firstborn son, and Joseph was certainly not that. As the eleventh son, his natural place in the family was that he would bow down to one of his brothers; it certainly would never be the other way around - at least not naturally. Why was Joseph so bold? Or was he merely a brash young man who wanted to irritate his brothers? Joseph was neither one of these. He was an obedient, earnest young man who obviously believed his dream was in line with God's will for his family. He could not possibly know the way in which this dream would actually come to pass many years later. I believe he told the dream as an act of faith on his part. In this sense, Joseph was a prophet. He was foretelling something that would come true at some future time, if he indeed was a prophet of God. This was God's method of showing us today whether one was a prophet or not; if the thing foretold came true, then the one who told it beforehand was considered a prophet. If it did not come true, he was not a prophet. Seems like a simple system, doesn't it? Joseph was not trying to qualify as a prophet; he was simply trying to be true to what he believed God has showed him.

The fact remains that Joseph prophesied. What he dreamed came to pass - later. He had many hard times to go through - as did his family - before circumstances would show that what he had no natural right to expect was in fact exactly what would happen. In fact, the circumstance of his telling his brothers the dream would be one of the circumstances that would further its eventual fulfillment. His brothers were so enraged by his boldness in declaring that he would rule over them that they began to look for opportunities to get rid of him. Joseph was not trying to irritate his family; he was simply trying to show them God's plan for them. They did not want God's plan for them; they wanted their own way! Joseph was a spiritually minded young man who already knew that God's way was the best way, even when it did not naturally seem so. He desired to be in God's will above all other things in his life. Would he have chosen the hard way that lay before him to do that if he had a choice? Probably not. He was going to be persecuted, left for dead, sold into captivity, wrongly accused and unjustly punished, imprisoned for things he did not do - and the end result of all that was so that his dream would come true. Was that so Joseph could feel vindicated and powerful? No, it was all going to be done to preserve his family and further them on their way to their destiny as a nation of God that would finally inherit the Land God Promised Abraham. Why should Joseph have to suffer for his brethren - his family? In answering this, we must understand that he was typical of the Lord Jesus Christ, Who would also suffer and die so that His brethren might be delivered from sin's bondage and inherit God's promises. Was it worth it? Yes, and He willingly suffered the same kinds of things Joseph would suffer - except He would die to deliver His brethren. Joseph didn't die, but he did deliver his family according to God's will.

I pray that we may consider how much Jesus suffered for us today, and be willing to suffer for His sake if need be.

The Strength of Grace

"...And Joseph went after his brethren, and found them in Dothan. And when they saw him afar off, even before he came near unto them, they conspired against him to slay him. And they said one to

JOSEPH: A MAN FOR WHOM GOD MEANT GOOD

another, Behold, this dreamer cometh. Come now therefore, and let us slay him, and cast him into some pit, and we will say, Some evil beast hath devoured him: and we shall see what will become of his dreams." Genesis 37:17-20

It is hard for us to have to look at the condition of man that leads him to plot and plan to kill another human being. Our newspapers and other media are full of these kinds of stories every day. So why did God choose to record such things in His word? Many people seem to think that the Bible ought to be full of kinder, gentler things; yet, again and again, Scripture shows us such scenes as this one. There is a reason. We will never understand the depths and fullness of God's grace unless we first get a clear picture of man's depraved nature. Without God, man is totally depraved. The word means that there is not one spark of goodness present, and there is no action outside the bounds of possibility that one in this condition is not capable of performing - even the killing of his own flesh and blood simply because of jealousy. Why do you think we are so curious about what makes a serial killer "tick"? There are countless documentaries about men and women who have killed again and again, seemingly without any trace of remorse or guilt. They do so because of this very thing - their depraved nature. That seems to be what was driving Joseph's brothers to plot his death.

Now, before we begin to think that such an act could not possibly be within the realm of what we would ever do, let us pause and remember, "There, but for the grace of God, go I." When we see this, we can better understand the scene that was unfolding in Joseph's life. His brothers did not care what God might think about their little scheme; they did not stop and consider if this was the right thing to do or not. They simply acted according to their nature. But so did God. He acted according to His nature. In fact, there is a common saying that is true of such a thing, "They meant it for evil, but God meant it for good." God does not cause men to conceive or commit evil deeds; but He is able to use their evil deeds to further the cause of His eventual good. Here is another thing, God does not allow the depraved nature of man - a nature that does not love Him nor seek Him nor even believe He exists - to stop His gracious purpose to save His people. He is able to deliver through, and in spite of, any obstacle a man might think he is putting in the way. In Joseph's case, the Lord was going to use Joseph's brothers' hatred for him to provide the very means of their eventual deliverance. They had an appointment coming later in which they would have to see that, even though they did what they did because they hated Joseph, the Lord would use that to allow Joseph to be the source of their deliverance from certain death. God's grace is stronger than man's depravity.

I pray that we will praise the Lord today for delivering us from our depraved, sinful nature and for preserving us in the bonds of His eternal grace.

Sold Into Bondage

"And the Midianites sold him into Egypt unto Potiphar, an officer of Pharaoh's, and captain of the guard." Genesis 37:36

There is a term in the Bible - firstfruits - that refers to the first of something of which there will be more. Most often it refers to something of which there will be many more. Joseph, in this fashion, was the firstfruits of Israel who went into bondage in Egypt. He would not be the last; there would be many more. The concept of firstfruits has more to do with quality than with quantity, however. As the firstfruits of Israel, Joseph's life would be hard for some time to come, and he would know the bitter taste of betrayal again and again. Still, he would eventually become the catalyst for the rest of his father's family to come into Egypt. They would come as guests who escaped the threat of famine ending their lives and snuffing out the future hope of inheriting the promises of Abraham, Isaac, and Jacob. How did

JOSEPH: A MAN FOR WHOM GOD MEANT GOOD

Joseph become Israel's firstfruits? His brothers changed their minds about killing him and sold him to a band of nomadic Midianites, also called Ishmaelites, instead. The brothers did not have a change of heart about getting rid of Joseph; they simply had a change of mind and method. The eldest brother, Judah, decided that they should not have Joseph's blood on their hands, so they threw him into a pit and would have left him to die; but one of the more practical brothers saw the Ishmaelites and knew they were slave-traders who would give them money for Joseph - they might as well make a profit from their evil deed. They drew him up out of the pit to sell to the Ishmaelites, soiled his coat with the blood of an animal, and let their father draw the conclusion that a wild animal had killed Joseph. Their mission was accomplished and they no doubt thought they had heard the last of Joseph.

The Ishmaelites decided to turn a quick profit and sold Joseph to a man named Potiphar, who was captain of the Pharaoh's guard. It is here that Joseph became the firstfruits of Israel's centuries-long sojourn in Egypt. He did not know this, and certainly no other member of Jacob's family knew it; but God knew it. He had special plans for Joseph, and for all of Israel through Joseph. He was their forerunner. It is here that many would stop and try to apply some rule or measure of fairness to this situation. Was it fair that his brothers treated Joseph so miserably? Was it fair that they sold him into slavery? Was it fair that he would only see the Land of Promise once more before he died? Was it fair that he was going to be terribly mistreated by his Egyptian master? No! No! A thousand times, No! Through no fault of his own, Joseph's life was forever changed. Instead of growing up as his father's favorite son, Joseph was going to grow up as a bond slave. Rather than basking in the good things that accompanied God's promises to Abraham, Isaac, and Jacob, he was no doubt convinced that he would never see his family again. But the ultimate purpose God had for Joseph was going to be accomplished through all the circumstances that attended these events of what we would call unfair treatment.

Was the fact that he was sold into bondage a good thing? No! At least it was not good at face value. That is where we must trust God. When events and circumstances in our lives seem unfair and life-changing when we want to stay right where we are, we need to try to remember that God may very well be using the present circumstances to move us to where He will ultimately use us for His glory and our good. We would have never gone to that place on our own, even if we understood that our present "pain" was going to lead to future gain. God is gracious to be with us as we go through the troubled waters of life, just as He was surely with Joseph as he was sold into bondage.

I pray that we may remember today that our God knows the end from the beginning. What may seem like unfruitful bondage to us may be the opening up of our lives as firstfruits of blessing to many others who will come after us.

The Blessing of the Lord

"And it came to pass from the time that he had made him overseer in his house, and over all that he had, that the LORD blessed the Egyptian's house for Joseph's sake; and the blessing of the LORD was upon all that he had in the house, and in the field. And he left all that he had in Joseph's hand; and he knew not aught he had, save the bread which he did eat. And Joseph was a goodly person, and well favored." Genesis 39:5-6

Even in captivity, God's people may prosper. The great-grandson of Abraham had been sold into bondage, but God was still with him. In fact, it became so obvious that the Lord prospered everything that Joseph set his hand to do that his master could not help but take notice and act to profit himself with the gift his slave enjoyed. At least that was probably the prime motivation for Potiphar to make Joseph overseer - steward - over Potiphar's house. This was no small job. The term "house" as used here actually meant all of Potiphar's personal

JOSEPH: A MAN FOR WHOM GOD MEANT GOOD

worldly goods, and he was no doubt a rich man. What was it that Potiphar saw in Joseph? Did he see the depth of his godly character and moral excellence? Probably not at first. It is more likely that Potiphar saw in Joseph's prosperity the opportunity to use what he thought was Joseph's keen business sense to increase his own wealth. It is highly unlikely that he sought to gain God's blessings for himself through Joseph. Yet that is exactly what happened. The LORD blessed the Egyptian's house for Joseph's sake. Not for Potiphar's kindness - for he had not likely shown much of that; neither for Potiphar's desire to advance Joseph because he was such a faithful servant - he was not nearly that unselfish; instead, the blessing of the Lord was upon Potiphar's house purely for Joseph's sake. The Lord was blessing Joseph, and that "overflowed" to the good of Potiphar's house. To bring this into modern perspective, let us consider why God is blessing America (if he indeed is still blessing her.) There can be only one reason, and truly there has always been only one reason. He is blessing her for the sake of His people. He has preserved America from her establishment as a nation until this present hour simply because He has blessed His people; and in blessing them, America has profited.

However, there is another aspect of Joseph's situation that we should be aware of. As God blessed Joseph, Potiphar began to trust him more and more, finally putting all he had in Joseph's hand to the point that Potiphar did not even know the extent of his worldly goods. He simply trusted Joseph and knew that whatever he set his hand to do would prosper. It was in that position of power over all that Potiphar had that lust and jealousy became Joseph's downfall. Not because Joseph succumbed to lust and jealousy - he did not; instead, those around him who desired to use him to satisfy their own lusts would cause his downfall. Joseph was a godly man. When Potiphar's wife desired to have Joseph, he refused her advances. Joseph showed his adherence to certain "laws" that ought to guide every child of God: First, the law of faithfulness to what is right (Joseph honored the fact that Potiphar had fully trusted him with all he had). Second, the law of chastity (even in the new Testament, the sin of fornication is shown to be an odious sin that has great social, moral, and spiritual consequences). Third, the law of piety (Joseph believed that such a thing would be a sin against God - and it still is that today). Wrongly accused though he was, Joseph's adherence to God's laws would land him in prison, all because of the lust and jealousy of those who had been blessed for Joseph's sake. The parallel to this that affects you and me is that Jesus our Lord suffered for our sake, so that we might receive blessings for His sake. It is also important to note that this setback in Joseph's life was actually advancing the ultimate purpose God had for him. Think about that.

I pray that we may understand in our circumstances today that we have been blessed for Christ's sake.

The Lord Gave Him Favor

"And Joseph's master took him, and put him into the prison, a place where the king's prisoners were bound: and he was there in the prison. But the LORD was with Joseph, and showed him mercy, and gave him favor in the sight of the keeper of the prison." Genesis 39:20-21

In Proverbs 16:7, we are told, "When a man's ways please the LORD, he maketh even his enemies to be at peace with him." It was evident that Joseph's ways pleased the Lord. They may not have pleased those who were jealous of him, as his brothers were; and they may not have pleased those who would have used him to satisfy their own lusts, as Potiphar and his wife each in their own way would have done. But Joseph's ways pleased the Lord. We can make that statement based on evidence. Once again, Joseph found himself in bad circumstances through no fault of his own; but once again, the Lord blessed him. Unjustly accused of wronging his Egyptian master, Joseph was put into prison. Not just any prison either. This was "a place where the king's prisoners were bound." Because Potiphar was captain of the king's (Pharaoh's) guard, he had Joseph placed in this "special" place.

JOSEPH: A MAN FOR WHOM GOD MEANT GOOD

As captain of the king's guard, Potiphar was also his chief executioner, so it is not far-fetched to believe that many of Joseph's fellow prisoners were there waiting their turn at the hands of the executioner. Whether Joseph was condemned to death we do not know, and it does not matter. God had a further use for Joseph outside the walls of this place of bondage. The time for his filling that purpose was still a ways off, and Joseph was going to spend some time in that prison waiting. In the meantime, the Lord was with Joseph.

He showed Joseph mercy, and gave him favor in the sight of the keeper of the prison. That is how we can know that Joseph's ways pleased the Lord - He made even the hardened jailor "to be at peace with him." It went farther than just a truce or a neutral position that the jailor maintained as far as Joseph was concerned; Genesis 39:2 tells us that, "... the keeper of the prison committed to Joseph's hand all the prisoners that were in the prison; and whatsoever they did there, he was the doer of it." Joseph was not what we might today call a "trustee," he was in charge of the prison! Now stop here for just a minute. Human reasoning will get to this point and ask this question: "If the Lord was going to allow Joseph to have all these privileges in prison, why did He not just arrange things to allow Joseph to be released?" We should be thankful that God's ways are not our ways. We might have released Joseph and stopped the advancement of the exact series of events that would culminate in Joseph being not just in charge of a prison, but also in charge of all Egypt! That is how God works - in the places you and I won't go, and in the circumstances we think are all wrong. It was by being in prison that Joseph would find favor with the man who would ultimately be the catalyst for his release and his being exalted to such a place of authority in Egypt. That was going to be where God would use Joseph to preserve Jacob and his family. That was going to be the place where the Lord would make a way for a little family of tribes to grow into a great nation. The signposts to the Land of Promise were being forged by the unfortunate circumstances in which Joseph now found himself. God's mercy is great, and His ways are past finding out! What about you? Are you in an "unfortunate" circumstance today? Stand still. Hold on. God may be allowing your circumstances to forge the signposts to a place of greater blessing.

I pray that we may look today for signs that our ways please the Lord.

Think On Me

"But think on me when it shall be well with thee, and show kindness, I pray thee, unto me, and make mention of me unto Pharaoh, and bring me out of this house: For indeed I was stolen away out of the land of the Hebrews: and here also have I done nothing that they should put me into the dungeon." Genesis 40:14-15

Imprisoned in a dungeon and accused of crimes he did not commit, Joseph was seemingly in no position to wield any influence or try to make friends of influential people who could help him gain his freedom; yet, the Lord is always making good on His promises. Two servants of the Pharaoh - his chief baker and chief butler - were cast into the dungeon and placed in Joseph's charge. Even with his "exalted" position in the dungeon, the Bible says that Joseph "served them." They had been men of great responsibility and influence with the Pharaoh, and Joseph ministered unto them as they waited in prison. They had offended the Pharaoh, and their stay was only temporary. He might free them, or he might have them executed; but either way, they were treated as servants of the king. Their greatest hope was that the king would forget their offenses - or at least forgive them - so they could once again assume their favored positions as his servants. They did not have any promise that this would be the case. In time, they each dreamed a dream, but they could not interpret the dream themselves. Joseph understood that God sometimes reveals His will in a dream, and that the interpretation of such dreams can only come from God. Centuries later Daniel, a distant relative of Joseph's, would find

JOSEPH: A MAN FOR WHOM GOD MEANT GOOD

favor with another king by following the same course - relying on the Lord to reveal the meaning of a dream.

Joseph interpreted their dreams. One held promise of a good ending: the chief butler would be restored back to his position serving the Pharaoh; but the other held promise of a bad ending: the chief baker would be hanged for his offenses. Joseph asked them both to remember him when they were released and to make mention of him and his unjust imprisonment to Pharaoh. They both agreed to do so, but the chief baker died before he could keep his promise, and the chief butler forgot. Have you ever promised to do something important for someone else but either missed the opportunity or forgot to do it? That is done all the time, isn't it? It seems to be more important when we are ones needing to be remembered than it does when we are the ones promising to remember. We love to think of ourselves as "standing on the promises," and that usually means we are basing our hopes and dreams on the surety of what God has promised His people. What about what God's people have promised Him? How often do we forget that? We would be devastated to think that God had forgotten even one of His promises to us; but it doesn't bother us very much when we fail to keep - or fail to even remember - the promises we have made to Him. Can you think of any promises you have made the Lord and failed to keep? It is uncomfortable, I know. Believe me, I know. But our promises to God ought to have the same importance to us as His promises to us. The good news for Joseph was that the chief butler eventually did remember the promise he made Joseph, and that would lead to his release from Potiphar's dungeon. He actually remembered at exactly the right time; the Pharaoh had a dream that he needed to be interpreted. The good news for us is that God will always remember His promises, and they will be fulfilled at exactly the right time for our ultimate good!

I pray that we may remember our promises to Him more faithfully today.

◄ MEN OF LIKE PASSION

It Is Not in Me

"Then Pharaoh sent and called Joseph, and they brought him hastily out of the dungeon: and he shaved himself, and changed his raiment, and came in unto Pharaoh. And Pharaoh said unto Joseph, I have dreamed a dream, and there is none that can interpret it: and I have heard say of thee, that thou canst understand a dream to interpret it. And Joseph answered Pharaoh, saying, It is not in me: God shall give Pharaoh an answer of peace." Genesis 41:14-16

Two full years had passed since Pharaoh's chief butler had promised to speak to him on Joseph's behalf. The butler, no doubt relieved that he had not lost his life, simply forgot all about Joseph when released from the prison. He forgot that Joseph had correctly interpreted his dream while in prison - that is until the Pharaoh had a dream and desired someone to interpret its meaning for him. Upon hearing this, the chief butler suddenly remembered Joseph. He then kept his promise to Joseph and told the Pharaoh he knew a young Hebrew whom he said was an interpreter of dreams. Having been called by the Pharaoh to come and interpret his dream, Joseph was careful to shave his beard and cut his hair to accommodate the customs of the Egyptians; and after he changed into clean clothing, he went to appear before the Pharaoh. As he began to speak to Joseph, the Pharaoh prefaced his telling of the dream by acknowledging his understanding that Joseph had power to interpret dreams. If that were true, Joseph could have probably named his price for interpreting the dream; but Joseph quickly deflected the intended praise from himself to God, "saying, It is not in me: God shall give Pharaoh an answer of peace." Once again, we see the true spiritual nature of Joseph: He could have taken full credit for having the gift of dream interpretation; but he would not do so. Instead, he gave the Lord all credit. Joseph knew that the only reason he could interpret dreams was because the Lord had some ultimate purpose for the dream's meaning being known.

JOSEPH: A MAN FOR WHOM GOD MEANT GOOD

It is a good thing to give all credit to God for all things. Without him we can do nothing. Unless He gives us the next breath we take, there will be no air. In the New Testament, we are taught to preface our every future plan with, "If God wills." Now I confess that using that phrase sometimes seems overdone, and those who use it may be so used to saying it that they don't even stop to think or consider how they will know if God wills such and such a thing or not. The real answer is that we should ask the Lord to show us His will in all things, and trust that He will do so. Our aim ought to be that we will not do what we do not believe is His will for us to do, and that we will do what we believe is His will for us to do. When our hearts and minds are set on that rule, I believe we can rest assured of acting in God's will more times than not. A dear friend recently said he was going to stop saying he would be in church at the next opportunity, "If God wills it." He said that he cannot imagine any circumstance when it would be against God's will to go to the House of the Lord! Joseph quickly pointed the Pharaoh to the only One Who could interpret his dreams - Joseph's God. Here is a lesson for us: when we have opportunity to publicly give God all the credit for something that has happened to us, we should do so; and certainly we should do so when speaking of the blessing in front of non-believers. As the Lord revealed the dream's interpretation to Joseph, he told it to the Pharaoh. That dream spoke of conditions of famine soon to come on Egypt, but it also spoke of preparations that could be made to stop the awful effects of famine. Seeing this through Joseph's interpretation, the Pharaoh would also see that Joseph was a man of great wisdom. Because of this the Pharaoh set Joseph over all of Egypt so he could administer the remedy God had revealed for the ailment soon to come. "And Pharaoh said unto Joseph, Forasmuch as God hath showed thee all this, there is none so discreet and wise as thou art: Thou shalt be over my house, and according unto thy word shall all my people be ruled: only in the throne will I be greater than thou" (Genesis 41:39-40). God's purpose to redeem His people was running like a well-oiled machine - it always does.

I pray that we may stop attributing our blessings to "luck," and give God all the praise for blessing us in so many ways.

Do What He Says

"And when all the land of Egypt was famished, the people cried to Pharaoh for bread: and Pharaoh said unto all the Egyptians, Go unto Joseph; what he saith to you, do. And the famine was over all the face of the earth: And Joseph opened all the storehouses, and sold unto the Egyptians; and the famine waxed sore in the land of Egypt. And all countries came into Egypt to Joseph for to buy corn; because that the famine was so sore in all lands." Genesis 41:55-57

Joseph had correctly interpreted the Pharaoh's dream: there would be seven years of fruitful wheat production in Egypt, followed by seven years of drought and famine. Joseph set a plan in motion whereby he required all of Egypt to set in store the overabundance of grain harvested during the fruitful years. In every city, there were granaries established and every Egyptian was required to bring his grain into these granaries. The stored goods were not only going to save the Egyptians when the years of famine came, they were also going to save many people from the surrounding countries who heard of this plan and came to buy grain during their own time of drought and famine. Included in this number would be a rather small family of tribes in the land of Canaan - Jacob's family. During the fruitful years, Joseph had two sons by the wife the Pharaoh had given him when he set Joseph in charge of this masterful scheme. Their names would be known among Israel for generations to come: Manasseh and Ephraim. The name Manasseh meant, "For God, said he, hath made me forget all my toil, and all my father's house." This was a tribute Joseph made to the mercy of the Lord in giving him joy in the land of his captivity. It is ironic that, in future generations, Manasseh's children's children would also forget the house of the Lord. The name Ephraim meant, "For God hath caused me to be fruitful in the land of my affliction. " Joseph, whom his brethren thought to destroy from the place of privilege in Jacob's family, would come to be well represented among Israel through his two sons.

Now, let's consider how what Pharaoh said to his people was not only good advice, but was also prophetic in telling God's people what will deliver them from certain ruin. Pharaoh commanded his people, "Go unto Joseph; what he saith to you, do." Do what he says without question. No doubt some of the Egyptians could have thought they had a better plan for the excess grain they were producing during the fruitful years. For goodness sake, they probably thought the fruitful years would last a good long while! But the Pharaoh knew that Joseph had better knowledge than the others. He knew the length of their prosperity, and he knew when the drought and famine would come; so the Pharaoh rightly said, "Do whatever Joseph tells you." There was a parallel event surrounding what is called Jesus' first miracle. Called to a wedding in Cana, Jesus accompanied his mother and others there. In the course of the wedding feast, the wedding party ran out of wine. Jesus' mother spoke to him of the need that existed and, seeing that He would do something about it, she told the servants, "Whatsoever he saith unto you, do it." That was good advice then in a natural sense, and it still good advice for us - both naturally and spiritually. Do what He says. Are times good and things going very well? That will change. We don't know when, but He does. Do we think we'll manage our own lives in the fruitful times and only seek Him to follow His advice when hard times come? It may be too late. If the Egyptians had not done what Joseph commanded them to do in the good years, they would have starved in the bad years. Because they did what they were told to do, however, they not only laid up enough for themselves, but they were also the means of providing for others who were in need. Their attention to "doing what he says" was going to advance God's plan to fulfill His promises to His people. Think about this from a spiritual standpoint, and resolve to, "Do what He says."

I pray that we will do what the Lord says today.

⊰ MEN OF LIKE PASSION

They Bowed Down

"And the sons of Israel came to buy corn among those that came: for the famine was in the land of Canaan. And Joseph was the governor over the land, and he it was that sold to all the people of the land: and Joseph's brethren came, and bowed down themselves before him with their faces to the earth." Genesis 42:5-6

Two things spread during the time Joseph was governor of the Egyptian granaries: The drought and famine spread to other countries, and word of Egypt's storehouses of grain spread to Jacob in the Land of Promise. There was drought and famine there as well, and his family's supplies were no doubt near exhaustion. It was at that point that Jacob commanded his sons to "get you down thither, and buy for us from thence; that we may live, and not die." At their father's command ten of his sons began the journey into Egypt to buy grain from the granaries that Joseph had established. Only one brother was missing. Benjamin, the youngest son and most beloved brother to Joseph, was kept at home. Jacob's fear was that some "mischief" might befall Benjamin, just as it had Joseph. It makes one wonder if Jacob sensed somehow that his other sons were responsible for whatever had befallen Joseph, whom Jacob thought was dead. At any rate, the ten sons of Jacob - called Israel - came to buy grain. To do so they had to appear before the governor over the land because he was responsible for selling to all the people. As they drew near to this man so important to fulfilling their needs, Joseph's brethren bowed themselves in deference to the governor's exalted position. Did Joseph catch the tremendous significance of this scene? Years earlier, he had dreamed a dream that they were binding sheaves of grain in the field and their sheaves bowed down to his sheaves. Now it was fulfilled! God had brought their evil intentions to come together in such a way that the very reason they had become jealous of Joseph and had sought to kill him - his dream of being exalted over them - had come true. Joseph was indeed a prophet in this.

JOSEPH: A MAN FOR WHOM GOD MEANT GOOD

This began a series of scenes in which Joseph spoke harshly to them, yet provided grain to them lavishly and ultimately without charge. They didn't know it was Joseph. The question comes to mind, How could they not know their own brother? Had he changed that much? No doubt he had changed, but it appears that they were too jealous of him to even know what he had looked like before. I would think that the last vision they had of Joseph before this one - where he was in the pit they had cast him into - would have been burned in their memories. Whatever the reason, they would not recognize Joseph until later when He revealed himself to them. There may be a parallel here as Joseph represented a type of Jesus Christ. Many people today appeal to those who do not know Jesus to recognize Him and desire Him in some way. They would not recognize Him in their natural state if He walked right up to them. Can you not appeal to them based on the picture of Jesus in agony on the Cross? No, they cannot grasp that picture naturally. How can one such as this ever know Jesus then? It is only by Him revealing Himself to them that they will ever know Him. When Joseph revealed his true identity to his brethren, they were convicted of their sins and sorry for them. It is the same with Jesus. It is only by His revelation of Himself that anyone will ever be convicted of his or her sins and repent. Then, they will truly and humbly bow down before Him. When Joseph's brethren first bowed down, it was because they wanted grain. They would later do so because they truly loved Joseph and were sorry for their offenses against him. If you have bowed down to Jesus, it is because He has revealed Himself to you and brought you to the place of loving Him for who He is - your precious Savior.

I pray that God's people will praise Him today for revealing Himself to us, so that we may know who He is and love Him.

God Sent Me Here

"And God sent me before you to preserve you a posterity in the earth, and to save your lives by a great deliverance. So now it was not

◄ **MEN OF LIKE PASSION**

you that sent me hither, but God: and he hath made me a father to Pharaoh, and lord of all his house, and a ruler throughout all the land of Egypt." Genesis 45:7-8

Do you ever come to the place that you believe you have just about figured out how the Lord works things out? Some people like a good mystery - a puzzle - that seems too hard for most people. Most like to try something like that so they can test their understanding and wisdom. We may think we know how God works, what His methods are, but we can never know all the details that come about from the small pieces of the puzzle that we believe we know. For instance, God is perfectly able to take some casual encounter you may have with another person today - just a simple conversation, perhaps - and use that to cause great changes to come about in that person's life. Furthermore, things that happen to you or me, such as a job change or change of location, may be coming about because God has something in store for our children, or grandchildren. Now, the question for us is, Would God use evil to bring about good? Not that He puts it into the hearts of men to be evil, but would He allow their intent on evil actions to come about and then bring something good out of it? Before we hasten to say, No! God would never do such a thing, let's remember a simple yet profound verse of Scripture that Peter spoke on the Day of Pentecost: "Him, being delivered by the determinate counsel and foreknowledge of God, ye have taken, and by wicked hands have crucified and slain:" (Acts 2:23). Did you get that? God delivered His only begotten Son to be taken and slain by wicked hands. He did not cause men to act in this case; they crucified and slew Jesus because it was in their hearts to do so. They were entirely responsible for acting on their evil intentions; yet God delivered Jesus into their hands. Why would He do such a thing? We can try to come up with an answer that will satisfy our curious minds or we can simply remember what the Apostle Paul said in Romans, "O the depth of the riches both of the wisdom and knowledge of God! how unsearchable are his judgments, and his ways past finding out! For who hath known the mind of the Lord? or who hath been his counselor?" (Romans 11:33-34).

Rather than wallow in self-pity or return evil for evil to his brethren, Joseph attributed his being sold into Egypt to God's providence. Had he not been in Egypt at this very time, in the very position that he held due to his "misfortune," the Children of Israel might very well have starved to death. They were now only two years into a seven-year drought and famine. The tribes of Israel had no grain with which to sustain their lives and the lives of their children. God had used Joseph's condition to preserve Egypt and He also used it to preserve the lives of the very brothers who had intended to kill Joseph and who had caused him to serve under hard bondage in Egypt. Not fair, some would say! No, not by human standards. It certainly would not meet the test of what is thought to be "fair" today would it? What about those to whom Peter spoke that day thousands of years after Joseph's revelation that God had sent him down into Egypt? Some of the same ones Peter condemned with the truth of their having taken Jesus and crucified Him were "pricked" in their hearts by what he said. They were convicted of sin by God's grace and would shortly act in obedience to Peter's declared remedy to what they must do to be relieved of such guilt. They believed, were baptized, and became members of the very group they sought to wipe off the face of the earth. They became followers of the One they had slain with cruel hands. Was that fair? Was it fair that God's grace reached to you and me, and that Christ died for us even when we were yet sinners? Was it fair that he quickened us while we were still in our dead spiritual state - rebels with no desire toward Him - and caused us to love Him and know He loved us? Not by most standards; but God's ways are not our ways. He is ultimately fair in all His ways because He knows the end from the beginning. Rather than try to figure God's ways out, let us praise the riches of both His wisdom and knowledge.

I pray that we may be able to assess our current situation today and consider that God may be using it to bring about great blessings to others or to future generations.

I Will Nourish Thee

"And thou shalt dwell in the land of Goshen, and thou shalt be near unto me, thou, and thy children, and thy children's children, and thy flocks, and thy herds, and all that thou hast: And there will I nourish thee; for yet there are five years of famine; lest thou, and thy household, and all that thou hast, come to poverty." Genesis 45:10-11

God's providence - His ability and His willingness to provide - is far too wonderful for us to understand. How He provides exactly what is needed for His people in exactly the right manner, and at exactly the right time, is a wonder to behold. We could recount specific examples from our own experiences, or from what others have told us of their experiences, where God has provided both natural and spiritual needs in a supernatural way. In the case of Jacob's family, He used the evil intentions of his ten brothers against Joseph. He used the hard bondage that Joseph endured and the false accusations of his master's wife. God used the circumstance of Joseph's imprisonment; and all these things were used to further His providing exactly what Israel needed to survive - indeed to prosper - at exactly the time He knew it would be needed. How did the Lord know? If we can understand this, it will open our understanding to many things, including how He can know what we need. If we need proof that God knew exactly what would happen, let us examine the witness He left Himself as far back as the time of Abraham, Joseph's great-grandfather, "And he said unto Abram, Know of a surety that thy seed shall be a stranger in a land that is not theirs, and shall serve them; and they shall afflict them four hundred years; And also that nation, whom they shall serve, will I judge: and afterward shall they come out with great substance" (Genesis 15:13-14). This record of God's declaration of the future shows an attribute that is sometimes disputed, though never successfully: God has foreknowledge of all things.

The word foreknowledge is only mentioned twice in the New Testament and its Greek form (prognosis) literally means "knowledge in front of" or "knowledge before." This does not mean that an event may or may not happen. God's foreknowledge is a declaration of a certain event that will indeed take place. It is sure to occur. When He told Abraham that the people who would spring from his seed would be a stranger in a land that was not theirs, God was foretelling the very event that would be brought to fruition by Joseph's words, "And thou shalt dwell in the land of Goshen." In our age, many people put stock in a fortuneteller or read their daily horoscope looking for someone or something to reveal the future to them. They think by knowing that they can avert disaster, or take full advantage of good circumstances. I don't know if a single member of Jacob's family thought of God's "prognosis" to Abraham of this very event taking place, nor do I know if they fully appreciated how events since Joseph's disappearance had worked to bring them into a place of preservation of their lives; but that does not matter. What God foreknows (and foretells) will take place. That is how you can know that He knows what you need, or even better, that He knows what is best for you. He is not limited by past, present, and future. He provides according to His foreknowledge of all things. As Jacob and his family would leave Canaan - the land promised to Abraham, Isaac, Jacob, and their heirs - many of them would never see it again. They had four hundred years as a people dwelling in a strange land to endure before the Lord would provide exactly what was needed, at the right time, and in the right manner. We may have a ways to go ourselves before God provides what we need, but we can rest assured He will provide.

I pray that God's people will thank Him today that His foreknowledge included knowing us in the fullness of His grace and mercy.

◄ MEN OF LIKE PASSION

What Is Your Occupation?

"And it shall come to pass, when Pharaoh shall call you, and shall say, What is your occupation? That ye shall say, Thy servants' trade hath been about cattle from our youth even until now, both we, and also our fathers: that ye may dwell in the land of Goshen; for every shepherd is an abomination unto the Egyptians." Genesis 46:33-34

A relatively small band of people left Canaan with all their goods and flocks and made their way into Egypt. The drought was great and their only hope of survival had been provided by Joseph's invitation. He arranged for them to come where there was sufficient grain to allow them food for the remaining five years of the drought and its attendant famine. Having been assured of the Lord that this was the right thing for his family, Israel (Jacob) began the hard journey, with great desire to see his long-missing son. God had reassured Israel that He would, "there make of thee a great nation." It would take a great nation to eventually go into the land of Promise and take the land from its inhabitants, as God intended. By no stretch of the imagination could the tribes of Israel be considered a great nation as they made their way to Egypt. Not counting the wives of Israel's sons, the Bible says there was numbered of them "threescore and ten souls." Seventy people - and this number included the sons of Joseph. Seventy people is not a great nation, but then neither would five loaves and two fishes feed a multitude of over five thousand in Jesus' day before He blessed it and increased it. That was what God was going to do for Israel, bless them and increase them. Two things would be important for this to happen: they must be situated in a place where they had room to grow, and they must be isolated so they would not mix with the Egyptians. Joseph knew how to take care of this.

Even though the Pharaoh had encouraged Joseph and agreed with him that Israel's' family could come to Egypt, there was a problem:

◄ 150

JOSEPH: A MAN FOR WHOM GOD MEANT GOOD

the Egyptian caste system esteemed shepherds in a very low place, even an abominable place. That is why, in a previous scene, Joseph would not even sit in the same room and eat with his brethren. The Egyptians abhorred shepherds. In this case, however, it would work to advance God's goal for them to become a great nation. Joseph made sure that they announced to the Pharaoh their occupation, knowing that he would send them as far away from the Egyptian population as possible to avoid clashes. So their place of residence became the Land of Goshen, which would become a well-watered, fertile place for their cattle to increase and for them to increase. Now, why is it that God's word always calls upon His people to separate themselves from the world? Are we to be stand-offish, and "peculiar" in our actions with other people? No, but neither are we to "mix" with them from the standpoint of adopting their customs and prejudices. There is supposed to be a marked difference between God's people and the world of unbelievers. We should stand out; we should be easily identifiable as followers of the great Shepherd and Bishop of our souls. Our problem with that is that we know the world of unbelievers does not like there to be that difference, and we don't want to be hated for our being different. A commentary on the Geneva Bible says this, "God permits the world to hate his own, so they will forsake the filth of the world, and cling to him." Remember, it was according to God's plan that Israel would grow by being a "separate" people. Their growth would eventually lead to their being made slaves in Egypt, and their suffering in that regard would cause them to cry out to their God to be delivered. Their hope as a people was in their being looked upon as being occupied with something the world abhorred. So is ours today.

I pray that God's people will be occupied with the things of God today, and grow thereby.

◄ MEN OF LIKE PASSION

Carry Me Out of Egypt

"And the time drew nigh that Israel must die: and he called his son Joseph, and said unto him, If now I have found grace in thy sight, put, I pray thee, thy hand under my thigh, and deal kindly and truly with me; bury me not, I pray thee, in Egypt: But I will lie with my fathers, and thou shalt carry me out of Egypt, and bury me in their burial place. And he said, I will do as thou hast said." Gen 47:29-30

Israel (Jacob) lived in Egypt seventeen years after Joseph brought him and his family there to preserve their lives. They prospered in the land of Goshen and saw their flocks and family increase significantly. Now the end of Israel's life drew near, and he began to make his final arrangements. His one desire was to be taken back to the land of Canaan to be buried with his fathers - Abraham and Isaac. As thankful as he was for the preserving effect of having been in Egypt, it was not his home; and he did not want it to be what most people call his "final" resting place. Isn't it funny that the grave is referred to as a final resting place? It is anything but final. I recently attended a funeral for an elderly person who had lived in another state for the majority of her adult life. But when the time came for her passing from this life, she requested that her family bring her body back to her childhood home to be buried - where her father and mother were buried so many, many years ago. The miles and the years that had separated her from her native country were finally laid aside. The land where she had prospered in making a home and raising a family was not where she wanted to be buried.

I believe that Israel wanted to be taken back to the Land of Promise for the same reason. Egypt was not his home; the land of Goshen was not his land. In fact, he knew and believed that Egypt was not the place where his family would stay. He remembered and believed the promises that God had made to his grandfather Abraham, his father Isaac, and to him: the land of Canaan was to be the place where the seed of Abraham would truly prosper. That was the place the Lord had first promised Abraham that his seed would possess. So Israel called Joseph, the only one he knew could ensure his request would be honored, and asked Joseph to enter into a covenant with him to take his body back to the Land of Promise upon his death and bury him with his fathers in the burial place Abraham had purchased so long ago. Why did he want to be taken there? I believe the main reason was that Israel wanted to impress upon his family that his hope - and theirs - was not in Egypt. The hope of Israel was to be the Land of Promise. Their deliverer was not the Pharaoh. Their Deliverance would come from the God of Israel. By his being carried out of Egypt, Israel became a prophetic figure of the coming deliverance of all his family "back" to the place God intended for them to be.

It is good to remember that this world is not our home. We shall someday be "carried out of Egypt" to be delivered into the glorious reality of our true final resting place.

They Shall Be Mine

"And Jacob said unto Joseph, God Almighty appeared unto me at Luz in the land of Canaan, and blessed me, And said unto me, Behold, I will make thee fruitful, and multiply thee, and I will make of thee a multitude of people; and will give this land to thy seed after thee for an everlasting possession. And now thy two sons, Ephraim and Manasseh, which were born unto thee in the land of Egypt before I came unto thee into Egypt, are mine; as Reuben and Simeon, they shall be mine." Genesis 48:3-5

There were a couple of things that Israel had left to do before he died. One was to pronounce blessings upon his sons. This was a custom of the time and place that was considered as important as the reading of a will is considered today. It set forth the last will and testimony, so to speak, of the patriarch of such a full and prosperous family as was

◂ MEN OF LIKE PASSION

Israel's. Another was along the same line, but was done less publicly. Joseph brought his two sons to his father to receive his blessing. What would have been Joseph's was to pass on to his sons. The reason may have been that Joseph was still bound to Egypt by the position in which the Pharaoh had placed him. Whether this constituted "an offer he couldn't refuse" is a matter of speculation; but there is no speculation that Joseph brought Ephraim and Manasseh to his father so that they might receive what was rightfully Joseph's. Normally, as the eleventh of twelve sons, that would not have amounted to much more than a few good words of encouragement and inspiration. In this case, however, Israel would pronounce upon Ephraim and Manasseh a double blessing, and much more. They would not only receive what was coming to Joseph, but they would also be considered as sons to their grandfather, and not grandsons.

By his declaration, Israel elevated Joseph's two sons to full sonship with his own sons; in fact, they were advanced to the "head of the line," so to speak. Israel said, "And now thy two sons...are mine." This was not merely a figure of speech; Israel was adopting Ephraim and Manasseh. Where they before had some family privileges according to their lineage through Joseph, they now had full privileges of sonship, even to the point that Israel equated them with his two firstborn sons, Rueben and Simeon. The truth was that their legal position was actually stronger than that of Israel's natural sons. There is a New Testament parallel where we, as God's adopted children, are concerned. John's Gospel tells us that, "He came unto his own, and his own received him not. But as many as received him, to them gave he power to become the sons of God, even to them that believe on his name" (John 1:11-12). This power to "become" the sons of God did not mean that their belief made them sons - God did that. Instead it meant that He enabled them to be manifest as sons of God. This is a legal term, and Paul strengthened the concept of the great privileges that adopted sons of God have when he told of God the Father, "Having predestinated us unto the adoption of children by Jesus

JOSEPH: A MAN FOR WHOM GOD MEANT GOOD

Christ to himself, according to the good pleasure of his will, To the praise of the glory of his grace, wherein he hath made us accepted in the beloved" (Ephesians 1:5-6). Just as Israel had made Ephraim and Manasseh accepted in the beloved, for Joseph's sake, from a natural standpoint, even so God has made us accepted for Christ's sake from a spiritual standpoint. Full sonship privileges belonged to Joseph's sons by the declaration of Israel, and full sonship privileges are ours by the mighty power of God!

It is good to "become" (bring glory to) our sonship, to the praise of the glory of His grace!

A Fruitful Bough

"Joseph is a fruitful bough, even a fruitful bough by a well; whose branches run over the wall: The archers have sorely grieved him, and shot at him, and hated him: But his bow abode in strength, and the arms of his hands were made strong by the hands of the mighty God of Jacob; (from thence is the shepherd, the stone of Israel:) Even by the God of thy father, who shall help thee; and by the Almighty, who shall bless thee with blessings of heaven above, blessings of the deep that lieth under, blessings of the breasts, and of the womb: The blessings of thy father have prevailed above the blessings of my progenitors unto the utmost bound of the everlasting hills: they shall be on the head of Joseph, and on the crown of the head of him that was separate from his brethren." Genesis 49:22-26

In a time of drought, not only is the land parched and in need of rain, but also the plants themselves begin to wither and fade. As long as that condition continues there will be little hope of their being fruitful, of new growth advancing, and of their having a healthy appearance. When Israel called Joseph a fruitful bow, he was stating that the evidence of Joseph's life was that he had brought forth fruit. Israel was not talking about Joseph's sons here; instead, he seemed to refer to

◄ **MEN OF LIKE PASSION**

Joseph's great success in the midst of almost continual adversity. In a sense, drought had been the constant condition of Joseph's existence since his brethren had sold him into Egyptian bondage so many years before. The drought in Joseph's life had not been just a lack of natural rain; it had been a lack of opportunity in the realm of one being able to forge the chains of his own existence. Instead Joseph labored under the chains that others forged for him: his brothers, Potiphar, the baker and butcher who were with him in prison. All these affected Joseph in a negative way, by all standards of what makes life bearable. Even the Pharaoh, who made Joseph ruler over Egypt second only to him, took away Joseph's freedom to plant himself where he wanted. Never in his life could Joseph do so; instead, he had to exist where others planted him.

Now, as Israel neared death and pronounced blessings upon his twelve sons, he stated the true essence of a life filled with spiritual victory over natural conditions: he referred poetically to Joseph as "a fruitful bough." He may have been planted by others and by circumstances he would not have chosen; but Joseph bloomed where he was planted. What allowed him to do so? His faith in God. It was his faith in God that caused Joseph to be a trusted and profitable servant to Potiphar. It was his faith that allowed Joseph to prosper and gain the full trust of his jailor after he was placed in prison because of Potiphar's wife's false accusation. It was his faith in God that allowed Joseph to save Egypt from starvation during a great drought and famine. It was his faith in God that caused him to arrange for Israel and his family to come down into Egypt. Two forces were at work in causing Joseph to prosper in every endeavor. First, God had a plan for Joseph and had allowed him to be sold into captivity for the eventual preservation of Israel's family. Second, Joseph was a man who exercised himself in faith toward God, no matter what his current circumstance might be. Not only was he a fruitful bough, but also he was like one planted near a well. Being watered prosperously, his "branches run over the wall," meaning that he spread out his influence for the good of oth-

JOSEPH: A MAN FOR WHOM GOD MEANT GOOD

ers. Israel spoke of Joseph as being greatly blessed by God Almighty, even though he lived most of his life separated from Israel's dwelling place. Finally, Israel transferred the blessing to Joseph that he had himself received as the God-favored son of Isaac. God was going to plant Israel (typified by Joseph as the fruitful bough of Israel) in the place He had promised Abraham, Isaac, and Jacob. Because of God's promises, Israel would be referred to as a vine - a fruitful bough - as well; and he would plant her in a place where He promised to put His name forever and ever. What about you? Have you produced fruit where you have been planted?

It is good to become a fruitful bough and "bloom where we're planted."

God Will Surely Visit You

"And Joseph said unto his brethren, I die: and God will surely visit you, and bring you out of this land unto the land which he swore to Abraham, to Isaac, and to Jacob. And Joseph took an oath of the children of Israel, saying, God will surely visit you, and ye shall carry up my bones from hence. So Joseph died, being a hundred and ten years old: and they embalmed him, and he was put in a coffin in Egypt." Genesis 50:24-26

Many things had taken place as Joseph, now an old man himself, looked back on the latter years of his life. Israel (Jacob) had died and Joseph had taken Israel back to the land of Canaan to be buried, just as he requested. His brethren had worriedly asked his forgiveness once again, fearing his retribution after their father's death; and, once again, Joseph reminded them that he had forgiven them and would take care of them. Joseph lived a good long life and saw his great-grandchildren grow up before he died. His life was rich in blessings toward the end! His father's family was prospering in the land of Goshen, and he was still favored by the Pharaoh and probably

MEN OF LIKE PASSION

revered by the Egyptian people as the one who had delivered them so long before from sure starvation and death. Life was good; but, as the time approached for Joseph's passing from this life, he ensured that the Children of Israel would remember that Egypt was not his final home - and neither was it theirs.

He "took an oath" of the Children of Israel, to be paid at some future time. "God will surely visit you," Joseph told them, "and bring you out of this land unto the land which he swore to Abraham, to Isaac, and to Jacob." Did Joseph know when that time would be? We could speculate that he did. Oral history was the tradition of that day. There is little doubt that hundreds of years later, when Moses recorded the very words Joseph spoke, he also knew the words God spoke to Abraham centuries before that. God specified the length of time Abraham's seed would reside in the "strange land" of Egypt. Abraham told Isaac, who told Jacob, who told his sons. Joseph was merely reminding his brethren of a certainty that he believed on the strength of two things: he believed his fathers and he believed God. The latter belief was undoubtedly even stronger than the first. As I grew up attending church regularly, I heard my grandparents and my parents express their love of the Lord and their hope of heaven. I believed them. But it was later made real to me, not by their expressions, but rather by my own personal experience of faith. I now know heaven is real because God has placed a hope of heaven in my heart! That was the basis of Joseph's making his brethren vow that they would take his body with them when God delivered them out of what would eventually become a land of bondage for them. When Joseph died, his spirit was immediately freed from Egypt and entered into the Presence of the Lord. He knew his body had to stay in Egypt until the day of promised deliverance; but he died in hope, knowing even his body would be delivered out of its representative bondage. So, Joseph's last act was to typify what the Apostle Paul would speak as precious reassurance to God's people centuries after this. "But I would not have you to be ignorant, brethren, concerning them which are asleep, that ye sorrow not, even as others which have no hope. For if we believe that Jesus died and rose again, even so them also which sleep in Jesus will God bring with him. For this we say unto you by the word of the Lord, that we which are alive and remain unto the coming of the Lord shall not prevent them which are asleep. For the Lord himself shall descend from heaven with a shout, with the voice of the archangel, and with the trump of God: and the dead in Christ shall rise first: Then we which are alive and remain shall be caught up together with them in the clouds to meet the Lord in the air: and so shall we ever be with the Lord. Wherefore comfort one another with these words" (1Thessalonians 4:13-18).

It is good to remember Joseph's life and reflect on God's grace and mercy typified by it - and also remember that He is the same God today, full of grace and mercy!

Moses: A Man Chosen to Deliver God's People

The Land Was Filled

"And the children of Israel were fruitful, and increased abundantly, and multiplied, and waxed exceeding mighty; and the land was filled with them. Now there arose up a new king over Egypt, which knew not Joseph." Exodus 1:7-8

As the Children of Israel became successful living in the Egyptian land of Goshen, two things marked where they were and where they were headed. First, the land they lived in was perfectly suited to promote their growth. Both in cattle and in children, they increased mightily. They were herdsmen, and the Egyptians abhorred keepers of flocks to the point that they wanted these Hebrews kept separate from them. Because of this, the fertile soil of Goshen was a rich land in which they prospered. So great was their growth that the second thing that would "seal their fate" was a natural outgrowth of the passage of time. They grew to the point that the Egyptian leaders began to take notice and also to fear their potential strength against those leaders, should the Children of Israel decide to pursue war against the Egyptians. This did not happen while Joseph, son of Jacob was second in command in Egypt. The reason was that the Pharaohs - kings of Egypt at that time - knew Joseph to be an honorable, peaceable man; and they assumed his people were of that same mind. The Pharaoh that arose, "which knew not Joseph," could have assumed the same thing and been safe in his assumption. But God was obviously in the details at this time and the time was becoming full for the Children of Israel to realize the fulfillment of the promise God had made to Abraham, Isaac, and Jacob.

God gave the promise of Abraham's seed becoming a great nation to him while this friend of God had not seen the fulfillment of having the son God had promised him. Still he believed God's promises. "And he said unto Abram, Know of a surety that thy seed shall be a stranger in a land that is not theirs, and shall serve them; and they shall afflict them four hundred years; And also that nation, whom they shall serve, will I judge: and afterward shall they come out with great substance" (Genesis 15:13-14). No doubt, through the succeeding generations these promises were passed down from father to son; still, the reality of the promises must have been far from the minds of these Children of Israel while they prospered in Egypt. Things were good. Life was good. They were becoming rich in earthly possessions and their families and tribes were growing. Why should they desire for things to change? The events that started with a Pharaoh who began to mistrust the Israelites was going to culminate in the fulfillment of God's prophecy He gave Abraham over four hundred years before the time of prosperity. Hard times were coming for the Children of Israel. Slavery and hard labor would be their lot for decade after decade, until they finally began to cry out for deliverance. Here is a lesson for us: we can foolishly think sometimes that we would be freer to serve God if we lived in prosperity. If the cares of life did not bear down upon us, we could dedicate all our attention and strength in service to Him - or so our thinking goes. The truth is that the Children of Israel would have been perfectly satisfied to stay in Egypt forever if prosperity had continued to be their lot; it was only when hardships became so hard that they could not bear them that they cried out, God heard their cries, and the plan He had for them as a people all along began to take effect. It is only in our dissatisfaction with earthly things that

MOSES: A MAN CHOSEN TO DELIVER GOD'S PEOPLE

we begin to desire heavenly things more. God was going to send a Deliverer to the Children of Israel, and He still sends deliverance to His people today when we cry out to be delivered. When we have had enough of trying to adjust to the hardships of life, we seek for His deliverance; and He is ever ready to bring us out of Egypt's bondage and set our feet on the path to the Land of Rest, which is found only in Jesus Christ.

It is good to compare our willingness to adjust to hardship with our desire to be delivered. Have you cried out to be delivered lately?

They Feared God

"And the king of Egypt spoke to the Hebrew midwives, of which the name of the one was Ship rah, and the name of the other Push: And he said, When ye do the office of a midwife to the Hebrew women, and see them upon the stools; if it be a son, then ye shall kill him: but if it be a daughter, then she shall live. But the midwives feared God, and did not as the king of Egypt commanded them, but saved the men children alive." Exodus 1:15-17

The Bible is filled with special characters, whose faith and works are well known, and whose names have been familiar to many people over the centuries. Others of similar note have remained unnamed. Then there are those whose names we are told; yet they still remain obscure to most people. Do you remember Shiprah and Puah? Not exactly household names, are they? Yet these two Children of Israel are named, their works are recorded, and the effects of their faith remain for us to rejoice in several hundreds of years after they walked such an important walk of faith. What did they do? They feared God, and refused to obey the orders of a king that they believed violated the will of God. The Egyptian Pharaoh set out to weaken the perceived strength of the Hebrews in the land of Goshen. He decided to practice what our society today politely calls "birth control." Of

MEN OF LIKE PASSION

course it was murder then just as surely as it is murder today. The only difference was that the Pharaoh did not have available all the modern conveniences for the gruesome act that are available today. He had to wait until the baby was actually born to see if it met the requirements he had set for extermination. His decree was that all male babies born to Hebrew mothers were to be put to death, and he ordered the "doctors" of the day - the Hebrew midwives - to perform the awful act.

There was only one problem with his scheme: the Hebrew midwives feared God's power and authority more than they feared the Pharaoh's power and authority. Shiprah and Puah went about their usual duties, helping Hebrew mothers deliver their babies; but, instead of destroying the little male babies as the king commanded, they "saved the men children alive." Such a simple statement, but such a glorious one! By their refusal, the midwives risked certain death at the king's hand; and when the king demanded of them why they were not doing as he commanded, the midwives said that the Hebrew mothers were strong in their delivery and always delivered the babies before the midwives arrived to help them. They implied that the Hebrew mothers were hiding the babies, and that is exactly what they were doing. We shall see in future days that their actions worked for good because it was in this generation that God was going to send a deliverer of His people from the hard bondage of Israel. A little man child born under the king's decree of death, saved by the midwives disobedient to the laws of the land, and raised to know the ways of the Egyptians as well as those of his own people had his life preserved because two otherwise insignificant women "feared God." Because of this, they were indeed "special characters." Their fear of God was not a fear based on avoidance of consequences, or fear of personal harm; instead, they revered the name of God and desired to please Him above all things. Yes, they were special characters, indeed.

It is good to assess our willingness to obey God rather than to obey worldly power and authority.

A Goodly Child

"And there went a man of the house of Levi, and took to wife a daughter of Levi. And the woman conceived, and bore a son: and when she saw him that he was a goodly child, she hid him three months. And when she could not longer hide him, she took for him an ark of bulrushes, and daubed it with slime and with pitch, and put the child therein; and she laid it in the flags by the river's brink. And his sister stood afar off, to know what would be done to him."
Exodus 2:1-4

In order to withstand the evil orders of the Pharaoh, king of Egypt, the Hebrew mothers in Egyptian bondage took every means to protect the life of their newborn sons as long as they could. One such mother of the tribe of Levi had a son whom she hid as long as possible. For three months she was able to hide the baby, a sort of miracle in itself. Anyone who has ever been around a newborn baby knows that it would be almost impossible to hide it if the circumstances demanded that the baby be kept quiet. Babies cry, sometimes even scream. They do so when they are hungry, sleepy, or need to have their diaper changed. Surely the king who commanded that every newborn male Hebrew child be put to death also had spies to alert him of the birth of these children. He wanted such children to be put to death so he could "thin out" the ranks of the Children of Israel, weakening their strength of numbers and lessening their perceived threat to his kingdom. He had already demoralized these people by placing them into the bondage of hard labor, treading the slime pits to make bricks they would use to build his great cities and monuments. That very fact heightened the risk such a woman as our "daughter of Levi" took to hide her child.

Why did she risk it? One little phrase tells part of the story: "and when she saw him that he was a goodly child, she hid him three months." A goodly child. Such a simple statement, yet so rich in the grace and mercy of God toward His people. God's word itself bears witness to the elegance and importance of this phrase. As Stephen, the deacon of the new Church in Jerusalem, preached to the Jewish leaders who would later stone him to death, he spoke of this very mother and her child who, ".... was exceeding fair, and nourished up in his father's house three months" (Acts 7:20). The Epistle to the Hebrews says of him, "...when he was born, was hid three months of his parents, because they saw he was a proper child; and they were not afraid of the king's commandment" (Hebrews 11:23). A goodly child, exceeding fair, a proper child. All these phrases have been preserved by the Holy Spirit to tell us that his parents somehow recognized that this child had a special purpose. How did they know? The Hebrews scripture verse (11:23), begins, "By faith," the child, "was hid three months of his parents." After three months they were no longer able to hide him, so the child's mother crafted a vessel - an ark of bulrushes - and made it fit to float upon the water. She then put the child in the ark and, "laid it in the flags by the river's brink." This was not simply her casting the child out to whatever fate might befall him; instead, she placed him in a location where she knew he would be found, and dispatched his sister to watch, "... to know what would be done to him." Unable to do anything else to protect the baby, she placed him in God's hands. Her faith was going to have immediate rewards as well as long-range rewards - both for her and for her nation. This baby was indeed a proper child - proper to fulfill his purpose according to God's word. This was the baby who would grow into a man marvelously used of God to deliver His people out of Egypt's bondage and into the Land He had promised their fathers, Abraham, Isaac, and Jacob.

It is good to realize that placing our children in God's hands is the very best place we can put them. He will guide their lives and bring about great rewards - both immediate and long range.

Drawn Out of the Water

"Then said his sister to Pharaoh's daughter, Shall I go and call to thee a nurse of the Hebrew women, that she may nurse the child for thee? And Pharaoh's daughter said to her, Go. And the maid went and called the child's mother. And Pharaoh's daughter said unto her, Take this child away, and nurse it for me, and I will give thee thy wages. And the woman took the child, and nursed it. And the child grew, and she brought him unto Pharaoh's daughter, and he became her son. And she called his name Moses: and she said, Because I drew him out of the water." Exodus 2:7-10

The Hebrew baby floated among the bulrushes secure in the ark his mother had fashioned for him, and his sister hid nearby at her mother's direction to see what would become of the baby. Was her hope that someone would find the baby? We can only speculate about that, but whatever was on the Hebrew mother's mind, it became evident what was on God's mind. There are many events in life that people will see begin to form where any positive outcome looks impossible, but where a seemingly miraculous turn of those events provides a wondrously positive outcome. Many times, the comments you will hear are, "Well, we sure were lucky," or "I guess the cards fell in our favor." Was it merely luck that brought the Egyptian princess to the water that day to bathe? Were the planets in perfect alignment, as some say, to bring about the circumstances that caused her to see the tiny ark hidden among the bulrushes? It is amazing to me that people would rather attribute such happenings to luck rather than to the providence of an Almighty, all-merciful God. No, this was not blind luck. Instead, it was the bringing about of natural circumstances to align with the sovereign, supernatural will of God.

Pharaoh's daughter came to bathe near the exact spot the baby's mother had placed her son. She saw the ark, opened it to see the baby, and immediately recognized him as an Hebrew child. She knew the commandment of her father, and knew that the baby's life was in peril. But "she had compassion on him." The next events that took place were miraculous! The baby's sister immediately ran and offered to find a nurse - a mother who had recently delivered a child - to provide mother's milk for the baby. The princess agreed, and the little girl - her name was Miriam - quickly went, reported the good news to her mother Jochebed, and they returned to the river's edge. Next, the princess allowed Jochebed to take her own child away to nurse him - and she would even receive wages for doing what was her heart's desire to do! The nursing period then was probably much longer than today, so Jochebed likely was able to keep her precious little child under her care for the next two years. As a side note, today's experts believe that the basic personality traits and abilities of a child are set within the first two years of the child's life. If that has always been true, then Jochebed had opportunity to establish and nurture those traits before she had to take the baby back to Pharaoh's daughter at the end of the nursing period. That day finally came, and the Hebrew mother fulfilled her promise by taking the baby back to become the son of Pharaoh's daughter. It was she who gave him a name that has been known by countless millions of people since that day - Moses. It meant, "Because I drew him out of the water." She was the instrument of Moses' deliverance from death, but God was the first cause. He had a job for Moses to do later in his life. Every baby born into this world is born to a purpose, but this one was going to be an agent for leading a nation of God's people to inherit the promises God had made to Abraham over four hundred years earlier.

It is good to realize that we have also been born to a purpose - born again - and that is to praise the glory of God's grace by living our lives according to His perfect will for our lives.

Who Made Thee A Prince?

"And it came to pass in those days, when Moses was grown, that he went out unto his brethren, and looked on their burdens: and he spied an Egyptian smiting a Hebrew, one of his brethren. And he looked this way and that way, and when he saw that there was no man, he slew the Egyptian, and hid him in the sand." Exodus 2:11-12

Moses grew up in the household of the Pharaoh as a member of the royal family. He no doubt had privileges and access to wealth and the splendor of the king's palace that you and I can only imagine. It is not far fetched to believe that he could have stood in line to be a principal ruler in Egypt, perhaps even the office of Pharaoh itself. Still, Moses knew who he was, a Hebrew, not an Egyptian. His heritage lay in the promises God made to Abraham, Isaac, and Jacob, not in the promise of wealth that attended his position in Egypt. He saw the hard labor the Pharaoh laid upon his Hebrew brethren, and it no doubt grieved his soul. He had not become a member of the king's household by choice; others had made that choice for him. The king had decreed the death of all newborn Hebrew children. His mother hazarded her own life to save his, and set in motion the events that caused him to be adopted by the Pharaoh's daughter. She raised Moses as her own son and gave him all the benefits of being in the royal household. There is little doubt that that he was educated by the greatest Egyptian scholars and received all the privileges that such great wealth could afford. But the New Testament Epistle to the Hebrews says of him, "By faith Moses, when he was come to years, refused to be called the son of Pharaoh's daughter; Choosing rather to suffer affliction with the people of God, than to enjoy the pleasures of sin for a season; Esteeming the reproach of Christ greater riches than the treasures in Egypt: for he had respect unto the recompense of the reward. By faith he forsook Egypt, not fearing the wrath of the king: for he endured, as seeing him who is invisible" (Hebrews 11:24-27).

MEN OF LIKE PASSION

Moses saw the burdens his own people bore as bond slaves to the Egyptians. They labored under cruel taskmasters making bricks for the construction of great cities for the Pharaoh. His heart was grieved for the people to the point that he killed "...an Egyptian smiting a Hebrew, one of his brethren." Moses hid him in the sand, but that event brought about the end of his life as the son of Pharaoh's daughter. By choice, Moses aligned himself with his people; but they were not aligned with him. The next day after he defended the Hebrew and killed the Egyptian, Moses saw two of his brethren striving together: "and he said to him that did the wrong, Wherefore smitest thou thy fellow? And he said, Who made thee a prince and a judge over us? intendest thou to kill me, as thou killedst the Egyptian? And Moses feared, and said, Surely this thing is known" (Exodus 2:13-14). His own people turned against him; and soon after, Pharaoh learned Moses had killed the Egyptian and, "sought to slay Moses." How could this be God's will? How could Moses' intentions be so honorable and yet his actions have such disastrous consequences? The only answer we can understand is that man's time is not necessarily God's time, and God works according to His time. Four more decades were going to pass before God's time would be full. Moses had some lessons to learn. He did not know he had lessons to learn. He no doubt thought he couldn't live among his own native people or his adopted people ever again. Scared, discouraged, perhaps thinking himself to be defeated, Moses, "fled from the face of Pharaoh, and dwelt in the land of Midian." There in the backside of the desert, Moses was going to be "schooled" in the things necessary for him to lead God's people out of Egypt: patience, humility, and faith in God's perfect will and purpose.

It is good for us to go the same school Moses attended, and wait for God's timing in our lives.

In Process of Time

"And it came to pass in process of time, that the king of Egypt died: and the children of Israel sighed by reason of the bondage, and they cried, and their cry came up unto God by reason of the bondage. And God heard their groaning, and God remembered his covenant with Abraham, with Isaac, and with Jacob. And God looked upon the children of Israel, and God had respect unto them." Exodus 2:23-25

Time marches on. Have you ever heard that phrase? It may be used to speak of the fast pace of the passage of time - such as seems to be the case as we grow older. Or it may be used to describe the sure and steady passage of time that seems to be unaffected by any event or circumstance of life. In the case of the circumstance in which the Children of Israel found themselves, time could have been more accurately said to be "filling up." The concept of the fullness of time is a Biblical concept. Hundreds of years later one of Israel's kings would write, "To every thing there is a season, and time to every purpose under heaven." Solomon was expressing the fact that time does not simply "pass" without meaning in the mind and purpose of God. He created time, and He uses it to bring His will and purpose to reality, even though He is not bound by time in any way. The Children of Israel's stay in Egypt was coming to an end, even though they did not realize it. God had made a promise to Abraham approximately 400 years earlier that He would deliver Abraham's descendants out of bondage and lead them into the land He had promised Abraham for an inheritance. Four centuries later, these people did not cry out as if merely on cue. They had been serving under severely harsh condition as bond slaves controlled by the Egyptian Pharaoh. Now, he was dead, and another king arose who would prove to be even crueler than his predecessor. The Children of Israel cried out unto God and He "heard their groaning, and God remembered his covenant with Abraham, with Isaac, and with Jacob." This remembering was in the vein of honoring, or delivering, what He had promised; and God was going to do so at the exact time He had told Abraham. Now, the Lord was going to turn His special attention on Israel and set in motion the wonderful purpose He had for them.

Time moved on for Moses as well. He escaped Egypt under threat of death after having killed an Egyptian who smote one of Moses' Hebrew brethren. He fled to Midian, where he married a Midianite woman who bore him a son. Almost forty years passed while this former Hebrew raised as an Egyptian prince worked as a shepherd of his father-in-law's sheep in the land of Midian. He learned the rugged terrain of the Sinai desert as well as the "landscape" of how to patiently lead sheep away from danger and toward the places where they could find the food and water necessary for their continued existence. Moses spent forty years in Egypt, and he had spent almost forty years in Midian; now, the ultimate purpose God had for his life was about to be fulfilled. His "time" - his purpose - was almost full. Moses was raised a prince for the first half of his life, but he had spent the last half up to this point learning how to serve. It may seem a strange concept to say that a man would serve sheep, but that is exactly what a good shepherd does: he gives his life for the sheep, giving over every moment of every day to provide good things for them. That is exactly what Jesus would later say of Himself: "I am the good shepherd: the good shepherd giveth his life for the sheep" (John 10:11). As the fullness of Moses' time and the fullness of his brethren in Egypt's time drew very near, the Lord was bringing about His purpose to deliver the descendants of Abraham, Isaac, and Jacob from Egyptian bondage unto the land of Canaan - that good land he had promised they would inherit. Yes, time may march on, but it always marches to the beat of the Master Timekeeper.

It is good to encourage ourselves that our time is in the everlasting and eternal safety of God's hands.

MOSES: A MAN CHOSEN TO DELIVER GOD'S PEOPLE

Holy Ground

"And when the LORD saw that he turned aside to see, God called unto him out of the midst of the bush, and said, Moses, Moses. And he said, Here am I. And he said, Draw not nigh hither: put off thy shoes from off thy feet, for the place whereon thou standest is holy ground." Exodus 3:4-5

In the course of his duties as the shepherd of his father-in-law's sheep, Moses found himself at a place called Mt. Horeb, also called the mountain of God. There he saw a peculiar site. On the side of the mountain he saw a bush that was on fire - a burning bush - and went closer to see what it was all about. Men have tried to explain this phenomenon by natural means, even saying that there exists in that part of the world a plant that contains so much oil that the heat of an intense sunny day could have set it aflame. Sounds reasonable, doesn't it? The only problem is that any attempt to explain this sight by natural means ignores the clearly supernatural aspects: The full explanation tells us the source of the flame: "And the angel of the LORD appeared unto him in a flame of fire out of the midst of a bush: and he looked, and, behold, the bush burned with fire, and the bush was not consumed" (Exodus 3:2). The angel of the Lord appeared from the midst of the flame. This was not merely a visual experience for Moses, because the angel of the Lord had a message for him. Today, in my home newspaper there was a story about a woman who said she saw a vision of a woman holding an owl in a tree in her back yard. People want to see "signs" and then make up their own non-threatening stories about what those signs could mean. God's word clearly tells us the purpose of angels: "Are they not all ministering spirits, sent forth to minister for them who shall be heirs of salvation?" (Hebrews 1:14). Angelic appearances are always directed and purposeful. The very word angel means "bearer of news," and God's angels bear news of His good purpose and sovereign will to minister these things to His people - the heirs of salvation.

MEN OF LIKE PASSION

Moses heard the message the angel of the Lord ministered to him. This news was specific. The angel did not make some general pronouncement to be heard by whoever might happen by. Instead, the angel spoke specifically, "Moses, Moses." The angel called and Moses answered. That is a central theme of Scripture: God calls, and His people answer. Moses said, "Here am I." The Lord knew where Moses was, and the angel of the Lord knew where he was. Moses, by his answer, was showing that he knew where he was. He was in the presence of the Presence of God. Many years later it would be said of the Lord's relationship with Moses and His people that, "In all their affliction he was afflicted, and the angel of his presence saved them: in his love and in his pity he redeemed them; and he bore them, and carried them all the days of old" (Isaiah 63:9). Being in God's Presence is not a casual thing. The angel said, "Draw not nigh hither: put off thy shoes from off thy feet, for the place whereon thou standest is holy ground." There was nothing holy about the dirt upon which Moses stood, and the spot where the bush burned was not inherently holy. What was holy was the purpose of God about to be pronounced - His sovereign will to redeem Israel from Egyptian bondage and deliver them to the land He had promised to Abraham, Isaac, and Jacob. Moses was included in God's purpose to save - he stood on that ground - and it was on that ground that God revealed His Name to His people for the first time. "Moreover he said, I am the God of thy father, the God of Abraham, the God of Isaac, and the God of Jacob. And Moses hid his face; for he was afraid to look upon God" (Exodus 3:6).

It is good to realize that we are still on that holy ground on which Moses stood: the promise of redemption from bondage into a land of perfect praise to the God of Abraham, Isaac, and Jacob.

I AM Hath Sent Me

"And Moses said unto God, Behold, when I come unto the children of Israel, and shall say unto them, The God of your fathers hath sent me unto you; and they shall say to me, What is his name? what shall

MOSES: A MAN CHOSEN TO DELIVER GOD'S PEOPLE

I say unto them? And God said unto Moses, I AM THAT I AM: and he said, Thus shalt thou say unto the children of Israel, I AM hath sent me unto you. And God said moreover unto Moses, Thus shalt thou say unto the children of Israel, The LORD God of your fathers, the God of Abraham, the God of Isaac, and the God of Jacob, hath sent me unto you: this is my name forever, and this is my memorial unto all generations." Exodus 3:13-15

As the angel of the Lord continued to speak to Moses from the midst of the burning bush on Mt. Horeb, He told Moses that the Lord was very much aware of the condition of the Children of Israel. "And the LORD said, I have surely seen the affliction of my people which are in Egypt, and have heard their cry by reason of their taskmasters; for I know their sorrows; And I am come down to deliver them out of the hand of the Egyptians, and to bring them up out of that land unto a good land and a large, unto a land flowing with milk and honey; unto the place of the Canaanites, and the Hittites, and the Amorites, and the Perizzites, and the Hivites, and the Jebusites" (Exodus 3:7-8). We sometimes sing a hymn entitled, "Jesus knows." The Lord knows the conditions under which His people labor. It may be hard physical labor and the bondage of slavery, as was the case of the Children of Israel; or it may be the hard labor of continuing to try to function in life after the loss of dear loved one. Jesus knows. The Lord told Moses, "I have surely seen the affliction of my people," and, in another place, "I have also seen the oppression wherewith the Egyptians oppress them." He was not merely aware. There are hard and unfair circumstances of which I am aware in the lives of some of God's people. I know these conditions exist, and I feel a deep desire to try to help. But I'm helpless to do anything about most of those circumstances. I know about them, but cannot do what I would love to do. Not so with God. He knows, and He is able to change circumstances for the better. That is exactly why He called Moses "aside" to see the burning bush. Moses was about to become the instrument through which the Lord would deliver Israel.

◄ MEN OF LIKE PASSION

Moses did not feel adequate for the task. "Who am I?" he asked the Lord. Qualifications to do God's work are not necessarily based on what we, or anyone else, believes qualifies a man. Certainly there are some things that may disqualify a man, but God chooses men to do His work based on His purpose and founded in His grace and mercy. After God's assurance that He would see Moses through the successful performance of this work, Moses made sure he could tell God's people who it was that had sent him to deliver them. Remember the question the Hebrew who strove with his Hebrew brother had asked Moses forty years earlier? "Who made thee a prince and a judge over us?" Moses knew that he needed to know God's name, for it was in that name that the authority and power to deliver resided. When Christ's apostles healed a man outside the temple in Jerusalem, the chief rulers of the Jews asked them by what authority they had healed the man. Their answer was that it was by the name of Jesus Christ of Nazareth, and that, "Neither is there salvation in any other: for there is none other name under heaven given among men, whereby we must be saved" (Acts 4:12). God told Moses His name: I AM. What a wondrous name! No one else can have that name, because it states the eternal character of the One who bears it. God told Moses, "Thus shalt thou say unto the children of Israel, I AM hath sent me unto you." He was also to say that the Lord God of Abraham, Isaac, and Jacob had sent Moses to deliver God's people. "This is my name forever," the Lord said. It is still His name: I AM. It was His name when Jesus told the Pharisee unbelievers, "before Abraham was, I AM." He is eternal. I AM is His name forever, and "this is my memorial unto all generations." What power and authority He has to save to the uttermost! In fact, He has all power in heaven and in earth. What God sets His hand to do will be done. He shall never fail.

It is good to remember that our Lord is the great I AM.

I Will Be With Thy Mouth

"And Moses said unto the LORD, O my LORD, I am not eloquent, neither heretofore, nor since thou hast spoken unto thy servant: but I am slow of speech, and of a slow tongue. And the LORD said unto him, Who hath made man's mouth? or who maketh the dumb, or deaf, or the seeing, or the blind? have not I the LORD? Now therefore go, and I will be with thy mouth, and teach thee what thou shalt say." Exodus 4:10-12

Have you ever passed up the opportunity to speak to someone because you didn't think you would know what to say? Maybe the root cause was because of shyness - everybody understands that. Some people seem to have no problem talking for hours about any subject, while others never seem to do much talking. Shyness sometimes can be wisdom exercising itself - a term the Bible calls prudence. We can be guilty of what I often refer to as "talking until we think of something to say," and we ought to never ramble on that way. The opposite is not good either. That's where Moses thought he was. He had probably become used to speaking very little, except as he directed his father'-in-law's sheep; but God told Moses to go speak to what was already a nation in terms of numbers and would truly become so in terms of God's plan and direction. Moses had already asked the Lord what name he should tell Israel had sent him, and the Lord readily replied to that. Trying another tactic, Moses began to attempt to argue with God that he could not do what God said he should do because he was, "not eloquent...slow of speech and of a slow tongue." Moses essentially said he had been always been that way, and he did not see the fact that God thought he could do what he believed he could not do to sway his own opinion. In fact, Moses went so far as to say that his lack of ability in that area had not become any better since the Lord told him to go speak to Israel, as though that fact alone should have made him into a great orator. He did not want to go and do what God told him to do, but Moses found that no excuse of inability is good enough with God.

"Who hath made man's mouth? or who maketh the dumb, or deaf, or the seeing, or the blind? have not I the LORD?" So asked the Creator of all things. Here is where you and I can learn a lesson that can change our lives: whatever it is that we are lead to do for the Lord that we do not feel adequately equipped to do, we should measure that feeling against this question God asked Moses. Who made you? Who was it that made your mouth and gave you the ability to speak and communicate with others just like you? Sometimes we build up an artificial level of required performance around God's directions to us. We, perhaps like Moses, have made it too big for us to perform - in our own minds - because we don't really want to do it anyhow. In Moses' case, we might excuse him because he was afraid of going back to Egypt where he had been wanted for killing an Egyptian. Or, we might feel sorry for Moses because he was truly shy and unassuming - God testified of him later that there was never a man who was more meek (humble) than Moses. But every excuse, whether for Moses or for ourselves, shortchanges the power of Almighty God! If He directs action, He will adequately equip the actor to perform what He has commanded. You and I can rest assured of that, and we have the evidence that God did for Moses just exactly what He said He would. He'll do the same for us.

It is good to do what God says do - without excuses.

Israel Is My Son

"And the LORD said unto Moses, When thou goest to return into Egypt, see that thou do all those wonders before Pharaoh, which I have put in thine hand: but I will harden his heart, that he shall not let the people go. And thou shalt say unto Pharaoh, Thus saith the LORD, Israel is my son, even my firstborn: And I say unto thee, Let my son go, that he may serve me: and if thou refuse to let him go, behold, I will slay thy son, even thy firstborn." Exodus 4:21-23

MOSES: A MAN CHOSEN TO DELIVER GOD'S PEOPLE

Why would God send Moses to speak to a man who would not hear him? In fact, God said He would harden Pharaoh's heart so that he would not let God's people go. Why? What natural sense did that make? It did not make any natural sense at all, because the deliverance of God's people was going to be of a supernatural nature. God knew the nature of man that was fully at work in Pharaoh would take credit for doing God a favor if given the opportunity. If Pharaoh was disposed to let the Children of Israel leave the bondage of Egypt, he would condescend to be the benefactor in the situation. God was not going to allow any man to take the credit for assisting Him in His work. He is still of the same mind today. Men will take credit for all manner of things if they are convinced they had any part in it at all. A man will take credit for helping God in things he has no part in whatsoever - including his eternal salvation. Listen to a man who believes that God saved him because of something he did. That man believes he is the critical element in salvation. He believes that God was willing to save him but unable to do so unless the man cooperated with God - unless the man provided that last, missing spark necessary to seal the transaction. Yes, Pharaoh would have taken credit for being the first cause of deliverance where God's people were concerned. God would have no part of that. He has said that He will not share His glory with another. So He hardened Pharaoh's heart, even though He sent Moses to speak God's righteous command to Pharaoh.

A strange thing happened here. The Lord called Israel His son, His firstborn, and He demanded that Pharaoh let His son go. The Lord was not just telling Pharaoh to turn Israel loose; He was telling Pharaoh that he had a purpose for them: to serve Him. God is all powerful and able to have the forces of the world deliver up His people - no matter how strong they think they are, and no matter how much stronger than God they consider themselves. It was true in a natural sense concerning Israel, and it is even stronger in an eternal, spiritual sense concerning His people that He chose in Christ. You see, when God called Israel his son, He was putting them forth as a figure of His only begotten Son, Jesus Christ. Not only that, God also told Pharaoh that he would pay a great price if he allowed his pride and unbelief to remain the agent that hardened his heart. Pharaoh hardened his own heart - God did not violate his will by using that fact to cause Pharaoh to take this situation to the point that there could be no doubt that God delivered His people with a mighty hand - supernaturally and without man's consent or assistance. That is one reason it is said of God the Son that He is able to save to the uttermost! He is a great God!

It is good to remember that God is able to save, and He does so without man's consent or assistance.

The People Believed

"And Moses and Aaron went and gathered together all the elders of the children of Israel: And Aaron spoke all the words which the LORD had spoken unto Moses, and did the signs in the sight of the people. And the people believed: and when they heard that the LORD had visited the children of Israel, and that he had looked upon their affliction, then they bowed their heads and worshiped." Exodus 4:29-31

Moses' two greatest reasons that he thought worked against his being the right man to go and do what God said for him to do were now overcome. He said he could not speak well and the Lord sent Aaron to meet him and go with him to be his "mouth." Moses told the Lord that the people would not believe him, but they did believe. Here is proof positive that, if the Lord is in any matter, there is nothing nor anyone that can stand in the way of the matter being accomplished. Do you believe that? It is an evident fact that the Children of Israel's delivery did not depend entirely on their believing God - He said He would deliver them. No, belief is not to empower God; it is to empower the believer. It is an evident fact that we will not act on anything we really do not believe. If God's people do not believe in

MOSES: A MAN CHOSEN TO DELIVER GOD'S PEOPLE

His power to deliver, is His hand shortened? Not at all. If that were so, then man would have more power than God. If belief were the critical element in whether or not God had the power to deliver, it would be a precarious matter, would it not? First of all, it is impossible to believe God - or even believe IN God - from our natural state. If God does not give us the gift of faith in Him, we will never believe. Evidently, the Children of Israel had enough people with faith to have it said of them that they believed.

What if some did not believe? Is God so weak that He cannot do what He wills to do unless men cooperate with Him? In fact, the Apostle Paul asked this very question about these very people, " For what if some did not believe? shall their unbelief make the faith of God without effect? God forbid: yea, let God be true, but every man a liar; as it is written, That thou mightest be justified in thy sayings, and mightest overcome when thou art judged" (Romans 3:3-4). Many people today are being promised supernatural healing by some man, based on his estimation of their faith being strong enough. What if God purposed to heal them, but was restricted by their unbelief? What confidence could we have in His power? Paul said unbelief cannot make the faith of God without effect. In other words, His determination - His perfect will - to do what He has said He would do will be effectual without the element of man's belief. It is man who benefits from believing, not God. Paul would later tell Timothy, "It is a faithful saying: For if we be dead with him, we shall also live with him: If we suffer, we shall also reign with him: if we deny him, he also will deny us: If we believe not, yet he abideth faithful: he cannot deny himself" (2 Timothy 2:11-13). Moses did not have to worry. God was going to be stronger than any unbelief in His determination and purpose to deliver His people. The fact that they did believe was simply a point of joy, that they were themselves ready to believe God - to live with Him, suffer (endure) affliction for His Name's sake, and "reign" with Him in victory as He delivered them out of Egyptian bondage. The people believed, and were blessed for doing so.

◄ MEN OF LIKE PASSION

It is good to realize that our unbelief does not restrict God's will, but it does lessen our joy. May the people believe.

Redeemed With Great Judgments

"Then the LORD said unto Moses, Now shalt thou see what I will do to Pharaoh: for with a strong hand shall he let them go, and with a strong hand shall he drive them out of his land. And God spake unto Moses, and said unto him, I am the LORD: And I appeared unto Abraham, unto Isaac, and unto Jacob, by the name of God Almighty, but by my name JEHOVAH was I not known to them. And I have also established my covenant with them, to give them the land of Canaan, the land of their pilgrimage, wherein they were strangers. And I have also heard the groaning of the children of Israel, whom the Egyptians keep in bondage; and I have remembered my covenant. Wherefore say unto the children of Israel, I am the LORD, and I will bring you out from under the burdens of the Egyptians, and I will rid you out of their bondage, and I will redeem you with a stretched out arm, and with great judgments: 6:7 And I will take you to me for a people, and I will be to you a God: and ye shall know that I am the LORD your God, which bringeth you out from under the burdens of the Egyptians." Exodus 6:1-6

Moses and Aaron went directly to Pharaoh to give him God's message: Let my people go. Pharaoh quickly stated would not do so. In fact, he questioned them as to who their God was, implying that there was none in Pharaoh's dominion more powerful than he! God's command to Pharaoh was to let His people go three days' journey into the desert to sacrifice unto Him, "lest he fall upon us with pestilence, or with the sword." Here was a strategy of judgment at work. God did not tell Moses and Aaron to tell Pharaoh this just to anger him: that is exactly what they were going to do - eventually. What God's stating this as His command was doing was to show Pharaoh that the Children of Israel owed Him their allegiance, and not any earthly

MOSES: A MAN CHOSEN TO DELIVER GOD'S PEOPLE

king. He had power to command them to sacrifice and He had power to command Pharaoh to release them from their hard labor so that they might obey their God. Pharaoh's dismissal of God's power did not lessen it one iota. His refusal to follow God's direction was a temporary thing. There would come a time later when he would submit to God's power - at least long enough to have God's ultimate decree come to fruition. God raised up Pharaoh, and He was going to allow his stubbornness to work long enough to condemn Pharaoh by his own actions and show God just in His actions.

Not only did Pharaoh not let God's people go, he made their lives even more unbearable. He took away their provision of straw but still required them to produce as many bricks as when they had enough of this necessary element to brick making. They had to search the land of Egypt to find their own supply of straw. Why would God start the process of their redemption from bondage and then allow that bondage to get even harder than before? Why does He lead us to follow Him with our whole heart, mind, and soul; and then allow us to suffer persecution at the hands of unbelievers for trying to do so? Do you remember when God's people were made to greatly rejoice at Pentecost and then soon after the Day of Pentecost were "scattered abroad," due to the persecution that "arose about Stephen" (meaning because of his being stoned to death for preaching the unsearchable riches of Christ)? God allowed them to rejoice as never before, then allowed them to have to leave that wonderful circumstance and be dispersed away from Jerusalem. It doesn't seem fair, does it? Yet, God's precious name was glorified because of that very persecution! These people would have been satisfied to stay right where they were if the persecution had not taken place. So it is in our lives sometimes. God "moves us" by many different means, but always according to His ultimate purpose and for His glory. The Children of Israel would accuse Moses of obeying God to their hurt, but God's plan was being worked out to their ultimate good.

It is good to praise God for moving us toward His purpose and by His grace.

God's Stretched Forth Hand

"And the Egyptians shall know that I am the LORD, when I stretch forth mine hand upon Egypt, and bring out the children of Israel from among them. And Moses and Aaron did as the LORD commanded them, so did they. And Moses was fourscore years old, and Aaron fourscore and three years old, when they spoke unto Pharaoh." Exodus 7:5-7

The Children of Israel were discouraged and angry with Moses and Aaron. The Pharaoh was also angry with them, but he was not yet discouraged. He would be soon, but not yet. The Lord had a measured plan of action, if we may call it that. A plan, in our minds, has the possibility of failure built into it. Not so with God's plans. They are as good as done before He ever lets His people know they are being put into action. His plans cannot fail and they will always get glory for Him. God gets glory for Himself. If we said that of a human being we would think it quite conceited and vain. Man assumes glory for himself, but he wants it to come from others in a positive way. All glory accrues to God - by definition - and He has stated that He will not share His glory with another. Even when men seek to bring reproach upon His name, God will get glory from that. He is just as able to use negative circumstances as positive ones to get glory for Himself. Here is a place we can get ourselves wrapped around the axle if not careful. Our fleshly minds will tell us that, if God will get glory no matter what, we might as well enjoy the things that reside on the negative side of that transaction - seeing he will get glory from it anyhow. Paul said this about that: "What shall we say then? Shall we continue in sin, that grace may abound? God forbid. How shall we, that are dead to sin, live any longer therein?" Romans 6:1-2. God had a purpose in subjecting the Children of Israel to the added hardness of bondage they were suffering, and it wasn't to punish them.

MOSES: A MAN CHOSEN TO DELIVER GOD'S PEOPLE

The reason for the increased hardships of slavery was so the Pharaoh would "fill up" his rebellion and hard-heartedness toward Israel. Some people might cry out that God just wouldn't do that; but He said He would. Four hundred years earlier, God told Abraham about this bondage for Abraham's seed in Egypt. At that same time, however, He spoke of the Land of Canaan, which the descendants of Abraham would ultimately inherit. He said that the Land of Canaan was "not ready" before His appointed time for the Children of Israel to inherit the Land of Promise. Why was it not time when God told Abraham this fact? It was not yet the appointed time because "the iniquity of the Amorites" that dwelt in the Land God promised Abraham was "not yet full." God was allowing them room to completely fill up their evil intents and acts - then His time would be full as well. Concerning the Children of Israel, God told Moses, "Thou shalt speak all that I command thee: and Aaron thy brother shall speak unto Pharaoh, that he send the children of Israel out of his land. And I will harden Pharaoh's heart, and multiply my signs and my wonders in the land of Egypt. But Pharaoh shall not hearken unto you, that I may lay my hand upon Egypt, and bring forth mine armies, and my people the children of Israel, out of the land of Egypt by great judgments" (Exodus 7:2-4) . God's judgments are just and right. He is long-suffering and merciful, but He judges sin. He judged Egypt's sin based on their stubbornness and disobedience. He did not "make" them get to the place where he would be just in judging their evil deeds; they (personified by Pharaoh) steadfastly refused to do what God commanded, so He was going to righteously judge them. He did so by bringing a number of plagues upon them for their disobedience, bringing them under subjection to the point they were willing to let Israel go. He would stretch forth His hand and bring judgment upon Egypt and her people. In doing so, He established His power and received glory for His mighty acts of redemption.

It is good to remember, "to God be the glory, great things He hath done."

◄ MEN OF LIKE PASSION

He Hardened His Heart

"But when Pharaoh saw that there was respite, he hardened his heart, and hearkened not unto them; as the LORD had said." Exodus 8:15

Moses and Aaron continued to go to Pharaoh bearing God's message to him. The Lord, knowing all about Pharaoh, told them that he would demand a miracle - a sign - from them to show the power of their message. Pharaoh may or may not have believed in miracles. He had a group of men called magicians who were able to produce what appeared to be miraculous signs. In fact, when God began showing miraculous signs - and some of them plagues - through Moses and Aaron, Pharaoh's magicians were able to produce versions of the same miracles. When Moses threw down his shepherd's rod and it became a serpent, so did Pharaoh's magicians. When Moses turned the rivers of Egypt into blood, so did the magicians. God filled the land of Egypt with a plague of frogs and so did the magicians. Throughout all of theses signs, Pharaoh was not turned from his disobedience. His magicians were able to duplicate Moses and Aaron's - actually God's - feats of power, so Pharaoh did not see anything truly miraculous in these things. However, that last one - the frogs - seemed to turn Pharaoh's heart softer, and he agreed to let God's people go. But when the frogs went away and things got back to normal, he immediately went back to his position of disobedience. It was after this that the Lord took away all semblance of the magicians' ability to produce counterfeit replicas of His power.

When the Lord sent a plague of lice upon Egypt, Pharaoh's magicians went to him and confessed that they could not match it. In fact, they confessed that this power must be of God. "Then the magicians said unto Pharaoh, This is the finger of God: and Pharaoh's heart was hardened, and he hearkened not unto them; as the LORD had said" (Exodus 8:19). There are two things in this we should consider. Do we cry out to God when beset by trouble, then go right back to our old ways after God hears our prayers, helps us, and grants "respite" from the trouble? If so, don't condemn Pharaoh - he also was just following his human nature. Next, let's say that the trouble comes back upon us. Do we, as Pharaoh, harden our hearts against God? Almost like a little child who determines to continue to do what he is receiving punishment for doing, Pharaoh went against the clear proof of God's hand upon him. His heart became harder. If there was a place for true repentance before this, it now seemed to be slipping away from him. In fact, it was going to take a number of further displays of God's power - including one final deadly display - to turn Pharaoh from disobedience to do what God so clearly told him to do. We, as God's children, can also find ourselves in the middle of "plagues" meant to bring us from disobedience to obedience. Thank God, He does so for us out of love; but the consequences can be just as awful for us as they were for Pharaoh.

It is good to thank God that He leads us to repentance.

Pharaoh's Final Refusal

"And Pharaoh said unto him, Get thee from me, take heed to thyself, see my face no more; for in that day thou seest my face thou shalt die. And Moses said, Thou hast spoken well, I will see thy face again no more." Exodus 10:28-29

As God began to show His almighty power over His Creation, Pharaoh stubbornly refused to do as He commanded. There were times that he said he would obey God's command if Moses would entreat the Lord to remove the various terrible plagues being brought upon Egypt; but once relieved, Pharaoh repented of his repenting and once again hardened his heart. The effects of the plagues grew progressively harder as swarms of flies came, all of Egypt's cattle died, horrible boils broke forth on the Egyptians' skin, hail and fire came, a swarm of locusts unlike any ever seen before came and devoured all

◂ MEN OF LIKE PASSION

in their path, and a darkness came that could actually be felt. At the end of these plagues, Pharaoh's heart was just as hard as at the beginning, and he commanded Moses to leave his presence and not come before him ever again. He was exercising a king's decree and for Moses to have come back would have meant sure death. It is ironic that Pharaoh pronounced a decree of death for Moses' disobedience of his decree, but could not see that God was about to pronounce a decree of death upon all the firstborn of Egypt.

There is a finality about death that we need to understand. That finality has to do with separation. Pharaoh decreed the threat of death on Moses thinking to separate himself from the threat of what Moses brought - or at least what Pharaoh thought he brought. He believed that if he did not have to see Moses, or hear the message he brought, all the trouble would end. Natural death separates its victims from natural life. God was going to bring death upon all the firstborn of Egypt to show He had the power over life and death. Here was a figure of His pronouncement of death to Adam as a just reward of his disobedience. God was going to separate His people from Egypt by bringing death upon Egypt's firstborn. Biblically, Egypt is used to represent sin, and God was going to judge sin by death - He would bring death upon sin! This is a very deep and heavy subject, but we need to know the depths to which our God went to separate His people from that which enslaved them! This was true for Israel in Egypt and it was true for His elect people bound in their sin nature. One final note: God pronounced death upon all the firstborn in Egypt, but He was going to provide a substitute for His people. That substitute was going to die in the place of His people! Praise His holy Name!

It is good to thank God for the death of sin and the life given us in His Son - our gracious Substitute who gave His life for ours.

The Lord's Passover

"And thus shall ye eat it; with your loins girded, your shoes on your feet, and your staff in your hand; and ye shall eat it in haste: it is the LORD's Passover. For I will pass through the land of Egypt this night, and will smite all the firstborn in the land of Egypt, both man and beast; and against all the gods of Egypt I will execute judgment: I am the LORD. And the blood shall be to you for a token upon the houses where ye are: and when I see the blood, I will pass over you, and the plague shall not be upon you to destroy you, when I smite the land of Egypt." Exodus 12:11-13

The tenth plague was about to come on Egypt, but God had clearly said He would show that he made a difference between the Egyptians and His people, Israel. That difference was pronounced. Not only would the firstborn Israelite children be spared, their being spared was going to be marked with a token so strong and meaningful that it still is known and spoken of today. The Passover is a Jewish holiday still today - although it is empty of its meaning - and is still observed as one of the three main feast days of Israel. The reason it is empty of its meaning today is that it was given to point to something that has been fulfilled in the Sacrifice of Jesus Christ for the sins of His people. The New Testament tells us that He IS the Lord's Passover - not a figure, but the true fulfillment of what the figure represented. It is important to understand that God did not simply excuse Israel from the effects of the coming plague - the death of all the firstborn. Instead, He provided a substitute for Israel's firstborn children. Each family was to take a lamb, less than one year old, without spot or blemish and slay that lamb. They were to eat the flesh of the lamb and sprinkle its blood upon the doorposts - the two side posts and the upper post - of the door of the house where they would eat the lamb. This was done so that they would understand that God made the difference, that He provided a substitute for them so they would not have to bear the penalty of His judgment against sin in Egypt.

Sometimes we see a car's bumper sticker that says, "Christians aren't perfect, just forgiven." I think I understand the reason people think they need to advertise that, but it does not nearly reach the depth of our condition as children of God covered by the Blood of the Lamb of God, Jesus Christ! Actually, we ARE perfect in God's sight, not because of our behavior or our condition of obedience, but because He provided a perfect Substitute for us Who perfectly finished the work of eternal salvation (the Father's will), and presented us to Himself spotless and without blemish. The Blood of the Lamb covers our sins and God still passes over them. He makes the difference, and does not depend on man to do so. When He sees the Blood, He passes over us - still today.

It is good to thank God for His making a difference in us.

What Mean Ye by This Service?

"And ye shall observe this thing for an ordinance to thee and to thy sons forever. And it shall come to pass, when ye be come to the land which the LORD will give you, according as he hath promised, that ye shall keep this service. And it shall come to pass, when your children shall say unto you, What mean ye by this service? That ye shall say, It is the sacrifice of the LORD's passover, who passed over the houses of the children of Israel in Egypt, when he smote the Egyptians, and delivered our houses. And the people bowed the head and worshiped." Exodus 12:24-27

Some people may think that what God required of the Children of Israel - to slay a lamb, eat it, and sprinkle its blood on their doorposts - was merely a ritual for that particular circumstance. It was not a mere ritual, and it was not a one-time occurrence. The Lord commanded His people to continue what He called "this service" when they occupied the Land of Promise. In fact, they were to observe it "forever." Why did God call it a service? The Hebrew word for service meant work, or ministry. So there was a work that His people were commanded to do perpetually - until the end. Now, in this case, what was spoken of was not the end of time, or the end of the natural world, because there was going to be an end to the circumstances under which the Children of Israel were to keep this commandment - until the Lord Jesus Christ kept it perfectly. Still, the service would last hundreds of years and was to be passed down from one generation to the next. They were to observe the service exactly as God directed once each year in what was thereafter called "the beginning of months," where the Jewish calendar was actually altered to have a series of twelve "religious" months. This service was important. It established the importance of observing this annual service in the hearts and minds of many, many generations. Generation after generation continued to "keep the Passover" by gathering in Jerusalem each year for centuries until the year that Jesus Christ kept it the last time with his disciples in an upper room.

Was it reasonable for God to require this service from his people? Every year they were to kill a lamb and eat it. Did they know what it meant? The Lord told them to be sure and pass along the importance of this service - of keeping the Passover - to their children. In fact, they were to be very specific in answering, "when your children shall say unto you, What mean ye by this service?" They were to make sure each new generation understood the need for this service to the Lord. The strength of their doing this was evident when succeeding generations did the service by keeping the Passover. Generation after generation selected a lamb of the first year without spot or blemish, kept it penned up for five days to "prove" its worthiness to be sacrificed, slew it on the fourteenth day of the first month of the religious year, and ate it with bitter herbs. They were diligent in keeping the service. Today, we are not required to perform acts of service toward God that are merely figurative. Our service is to be real, spiritually motivated, and Christ-honoring. We are to keep the service God has given us to keep "forever," just as surely as the Children of Israel were to keep the service He gave them. Do you love to keep the worship service? Do you believe it is important to let the next generation know what this service means to you? Does it bother you to miss a worship service? You will have to answer these questions, but each one needs to remember that the next generation is going to ask, "What mean ye by this service?"

It is good to resolve to keep the service of God - a reasonable service - in a better way that we have ever done before.

Not by the Easy Way

"And it came to pass, when Pharaoh had let the people go, that God led them not through the way of the land of the Philistines, although that was near; for God said, Lest peradventure the people repent when they see war, and they return to Egypt: But God led the people about, through the way of the wilderness of the Red sea: and the children of Israel went up harnessed out of the land of Egypt." Exodus 13:17-18

Finally, Pharaoh could no longer resist the power of God. After the death of all of Egypt's firstborn, he stood aside as the Children of Israel left the land where they had both prospered and suffered hard bondage. The Lord had shown His great power and determinate will to deliver His people out of bondage; but His purpose behind this redemption was not just to deliver Israel from Egypt. The ultimate glory of such a miracle was not in what was behind in their experience, but it was in what was in front of them. They were going to be delivered to dwell in the land that God had promised Abraham, Isaac, and Jacob hundreds of years earlier. The day they marched out of Egypt was the beginning of the glory of Israel, as they fulfilled God's purpose for them. There were going to be good times and times of extreme trouble ahead, but God was going to be with them. He would show them that time after time. Their job was to keep going. Even in leaving Egypt, the main thing the Children of Israel had to do was to keep moving forward.

God knew that the easiest, most direct route for moving forward was not the best way for Israel to move. Why? The reason was that what Israel thought was the best way, the easiest way, was in fact the way with the most potential danger for them. The most direct route was directly up the coast of the Mediterranean Sea, out of Egypt into Palestine. But along this route dwelt a fierce, war-loving people - the Philistines. The Lord knew that the Philistines would certainly attack the Children of Israel as they passed through their land. They might have easily defeated the Philistines because of the strength of their numbers - it is estimated that approximately 6 million men, women, and children left Egypt - but even strength of numbers cannot make up for a lack of will to fight. When they might have "organized" themselves and been able to overwhelm the Pharaoh's army simply because of the strength of their numbers, these people had remained subject to Egyptian bondage for many years. No, the Lord was not going to expose them to a test greater than they were able to bear - sound familiar? He has promised us the same thing. Instead of taking them by the easy way, He "led the people about, through the way of the wilderness of the Red sea." It would be along this route that they would learn to depend on the Lord, and some who would not do so would fall by the way side. God's way may not be the easy way, but it is always the best way.

It is good to walk in the way God is leading, knowing He is with us.

To Go by Day and Night

"And the LORD went before them by day in a pillar of a cloud, to lead them the way; and by night in a pillar of fire, to give them light; to go by day and night: He took not away the pillar of the cloud by day, nor the pillar of fire by night, from before the people." Exodus 13:21-22

Immediately as the Children of Israel marched out of Egypt God gave them a visible token of His Presence with them. By day, a pillar of cloud went before them to "lead them the way"; and by night, a pillar of fire appeared to give them light. From the time of Creation, God has separated the light from the darkness and made a difference between day and night. The daytime is understood to represent a period of time in which work may be done, and the nighttime is understood to be a time of rest to prepare for the duties of the next day. Whether by day or by night, these columns were understood to be the Presence of God with them. Was God in the cloud, or in the fire? Not literally, but the Scripture says that, "the LORD went before them" in these tokens of His Presence. He was not literally in the pillar of cloud, nor was He in the pillar of fire; but they represented His glory. In fact, the Hebrew word for this is Shekina - the glory of the Lord. Many passages of Old Testament scripture describe these two elements as God showed His Presence with His people: fire and smoke showed His anger against sin as he gave Moses the Law on Mt. Sinai. When He was well pleased with a particular offering under the law, fire came out to consume the offering. When the priests stood in the Tabernacle, and then in the Temple, and ministered according to His will, a cloud filled the sanctuary. These tokens of His Presence would eventually be seen exclusively in the confines of the Tabernacle and then the Temple; but as His people moved toward the Land of Promise, God's tokens of the glory of His Presence were visible to all.

Eventually, these tokens would not be seen in Israel, but now they could be clearly seen. The Children of Israel understood that this was not merely a token of God's Presence: this was the Lord. There is a big difference in our believing that God is with us because Jesus said that He would never leave us nor forsake us, and in our believing God is with us because we spiritually sense His Presence. This is something the unbelieving world does not understand: God is real. He is present right now as you are reading this - not in the words written, but in the truth they represent. We do not have a visible token like the Children of Israel had - neither pillar of cloud by day, nor pillar of fire by night.

We don't see these things. But we see Jesus. We see Him by faith, and He is the Glory of God. He is with us during the day and He is with us during the night. He leads us in the way and He gives us light. In fact, the word Shekinah means resting-place, or place of abode. When the Prophet Isaiah first spoke plainly of the coming Redeemer of God's people, he said his name would be called Immanuel - God with us. John's Gospel said of Him whom he called the Word - that He "was made flesh, and dwelt among us, (and we beheld his glory, the glory as of the only begotten of the Father,) full of grace and truth." He is with us, giving us the ability to go by day and night.

It is good to stop and realize He is with you.

Overtaken by the Sea

"And the LORD hardened the heart of Pharaoh king of Egypt, and he pursued after the children of Israel: and the children of Israel went out with a high hand. But the Egyptians pursued after them, all the horses and chariots of Pharaoh, and his horsemen, and his army, and overtook them encamping by the sea, beside Pi-hahiroth, before Baal-zephon." Exodus 14:8-9

Pharaoh's grief in losing all the firstborn in Egypt was replaced by intense anger at losing Egypt's slave labor population, so he gathered together his soldiers and chariots and horses and pursued after the Children of Israel. He intended to capture them and bring them back to Egypt. While we are not told what their number was, it is highly unlikely that the number of Pharaoh's total army was anywhere near the number of the Children of Israel. It took a lot of nerve for Pharaoh to think that he could round up the Israelites and march them right back to Egyptian bondage. Of course, a man with an ego as big as Pharaoh's is not encumbered with a lot of common sense and clear thinking. We know how obstinate and stubborn he was, even while the Lord brought plague after plague on Egypt to show that He had

MEN OF LIKE PASSION

power over Pharaoh. If that seems strange to you, just think how absurd it is for Satan to think he can usurp power over God. Think how much "nerve" it took for Satan to think he could tempt the Lord, Jesus Christ to bow down before him or to cast Himself off a high mountain! Even more absurd is the thought that Satan can somehow gain eternal power over even one of God's elect children! Pharaoh's ego convinced him that he could still withstand the power of Israel's God, but the Lord had other plans.

The Lord told Moses to have Israel encamp beside the sea - the Red Sea - at a place called Pi-hahiroth. With their backs to the sea, the Children of Israel appeared extremely vulnerable to attack. The sea was a barrier to their being able to continue their eastward path away from Egypt - or so Pharaoh thought. Natural barriers present no challenge to the power of God. What men think is a barrier is not a barrier to God. Even though modern day unbelievers have attempted to discount the power of the miracle that was about to happen by saying the sea was only a few inches deep, God was going to show His power in a wondrous way. When the enemies of God believe they have limited His power because of some obstacle that seems to hamper the possibility of Him being able to deliver His people, they show their complete lack of understanding of who God is. We can certainly say that of those who hate God. They are deceived by their own lust for power. But what about those who think to limit the power of God in the eternal salvation of his people? If there is some obstacle a man can place between himself and God's ability to save him eternally - even his unbelief - how is that different from Pharaoh's apparent belief that he had hemmed in God and His people by the sea? Pharaoh was going to see that there is no obstacle God cannot overcome in performing His perfect will. How much happier men would be, how much more glory they would give God, if they could see that this same principle applies in God's perfect will to save His people from the bondage of their sins. Pharaoh's obstinacy was going to cost him his life, and God was going to get glory from the miraculous show of His power.

It is good to remember that God can overcome all obstacles in our lives that seem to limit His power.

Stand Still, Then Go Forward

"And Moses said unto the people, Fear ye not, stand still, and see the salvation of the LORD, which he will shew to you to day: for the Egyptians whom ye have seen to day, ye shall see them again no more for ever. The LORD shall fight for you, and ye shall hold your peace. And the LORD said unto Moses, Wherefore criest thou unto me? speak unto the children of Israel, that they go forward:" Exodus 14:13-15

What do you do when your back is against the wall? Or, like the Children of Israel, when your back is against the Red Sea and Pharaoh's army is fast approaching to destroy you? The Children of Israel almost immediately began to accuse Moses of leading them out into the wilderness to die. How could they do that? Had they not just seen miracle after miracle that the Lord had worked to show His power to deliver them from Egypt? Where was their faith? You and I know that faith is a wonderful subject to talk about when you apparently don't need it. When things are going well, we talk and talk about faith. We can even look at other people's apparent lack of faith in their circumstances and wonder why they are failing so miserably. But, when things start to go wrong with us, when the chariots of destruction are seemingly headed our way and we can't see any means of escape, what is our reaction? The perceived reality of what we see overcomes our faith many times - at least momentarily. The Israelites "lifted up their eyes," saw Pharaoh's army closing in on them, and "were sore afraid." Have you ever been there? Well, what are we supposed to do?

First we are to stand still. It is extremely hard to quiet ourselves when disaster is about to strike us; but panic never accomplishes anything.

MEN OF LIKE PASSION

Panic leads to irrational actions. It clouds our judgment on what to do in our present circumstances. Now, obviously, if you're in the middle of the street and a bus is bearing down on you, you need to act fast! There's not much time to think, you just need to react. Even then, however, panic may freeze you in your tracks and bring about disastrous results. Moses told the people to stand still - settle down. They were to take their eyes off the approaching army and look to God. Moses said, "stand still, and see the salvation of the LORD, which he will shew to you to day." The next action belonged to God. The people could not deliver themselves until God made a way of escape. Has He promised that to you and me? In I Corinthians 10:13, Paul told God's people, "There hath no temptation taken you but such as is common to man: but God is faithful, who will not suffer you to be tempted above that ye are able; but will with the temptation also make a way to escape, that ye may be able to bear it." Once a way of escape became apparent, God commanded the people to "Go forward." God's path of deliverance is: stand still, see the salvation of the Lord, and then go forward. When Israel took this path, the path of faith, they were able to escape what seemed inescapable.

It is good to try out God's "formula" for escape: stand still, see the salvation of the Lord, and then go forward.

Walked Upon Dry Land

"And the waters returned, and covered the chariots, and the horsemen, and all the host of Pharaoh that came into the sea after them; there remained not so much as one of them. But the children of Israel walked upon dry land in the midst of the sea; and the waters were a wall unto them on their right hand, and on their left. Thus the LORD saved Israel that day out of the hand of the Egyptians; and Israel saw the Egyptians dead upon the sea shore." Exodus 14:28-30

This is perhaps the most talked about, the most recognized miracle recorded in the Bible. People who may not know anything else about God's word know the parting of the Red Sea. But this was not just a natural miracle - in fact, we might even say it was really not miraculous at all. Why? Because the same God Who created the heavens and the earth, the sea and the dry land, and every living thing upon the earth - all from nothing - is surely able to cause the elements of His Creation to act in any way He wills! Those who even believe in this so-called miracle (and there are many who do not believe it) act amazed that the waters divided at God's command. Paul, in writing to the Colossian Church, said, "For by him were all things created, that are in heaven, and that are in earth, visible and invisible, whether they be thrones, or dominions, or principalities, or powers: all things were created by him, and for him: And he is before all things, and by him all things consist" (Colossians 1:16-17). He was speaking of the Lord, Jesus Christ, Who Himself commanded the raging Sea of Galilee to be still. He Who created all things is certainly able to do with those things whatsoever He desires. Not only did He cause the waters to stand up, He also caused the wind to blow in such a way that the deep mud that would have existed under the sea was dried up such that the Children of Israel walked across on dry ground. The problem seemed to be that the same convenience provided them also was going to help the Egyptians catch them; but God's miracles are not one-dimensional.

The same miraculous event that provided a means of escape for God's people also provided the means of defeat for their enemies. As the Children of Israel reached the eastern shore of the Red Sea and the Egyptian army was coming across using the very same path provided for Israel's deliverance, "the waters returned, and covered the chariots, and the horsemen, and all the host of Pharaoh that came into the sea after them; there remained not so much as one of them." This was a two-part miracle! Now, let's consider the purpose for God's miracles: does He need to perform natural, miraculous events so people will believe in Him? No. He does not. In fact, the greatest miracles are not in the natural realm. The greatest miracles are changed lives. That is in the spiritual realm, and God is just as able in that realm as in the natural. He is the Creator of all things. He is able to overcome the natural curse of sin and death to save His people. Every element in the eternal salvation of His people is totally under His control, just as are the waters of the Red Sea and the wind that brought about the dry ground in the midst of it. There is a proper response to this: "And Israel saw that great work which the LORD did upon the Egyptians: and the people feared the LORD, and believed the LORD, and his servant Moses" (Exodus 14:31).

It is good to see God's miracles in our lives, fear Him, and believe Him.

The Song of Moses

"Then sang Moses and the children of Israel this song unto the LORD, and spake, saying, I will sing unto the LORD, for he hath triumphed gloriously: the horse and his rider hath he thrown into the sea. The LORD is my strength and song, and he is become my salvation: he is my God, and I will prepare him an habitation; my father's God, and I will exalt him." Exodus 15:1-2

Safe on the other side of the Red Sea, the Children of Israel looked back and saw the power of God release the walls of water to collapse and drown the Pharaoh and his army - the same walls that had formed the corridor of their escape. It was good to be on the other side of the trouble that had threatened to consume them just moments earlier. What a relief! What joy God's people can experience when we pass through times of great trials and get to the other side of them! No wonder they sang. It was the custom to sing the praises of the victor in that day. When a great battle had been won, the people would sing about the victory and praise the man who had led them into battle and helped them win it. This was the kind of song Israel sang that day. It is referred to as the Song of Moses, but it was not praising him - Moses merely gave them the song and they sang it. Another example of this happened many years later when David slew the giant Goliath. As he came back with King Saul's army from that battle, the people sang a song praising his courage and victory, "Saul has slain his thousands, but David his ten thousands." The people began to put their trust in David from that point forward. In Moses' case, he was directing the people's attention to the true victor - the God of Abraham, Isaac, and Jacob. They sang Moses' song unto the praise of the Lord.

Do you have a song to sing today? Has God given you any victories, and can you praise His name? He is worthy of your praise! The Lord is a victorious King. He has conquered His enemies. Many people are looking for a final, natural battle where the Lord will literally fight the armies of evil and finally, after such a long time, triumph over them. But God's word tells us that He has already done it! When Jesus died on the Cross as the Lamb of God, He won the victory over the power of sin. When He arose from the grave on the appointed day, He won the victory over death, hell, and the grave. Surely, the Lamb deserves a song of praise! Moses' song said, "The LORD is my strength and song, and he is become my salvation: he is my God, and I will prepare him an habitation; my father's God, and I will exalt him." Do you believe that Jesus has triumphed, with a victory far greater than the victory that spurred Moses' song? If so, sing His praises. As the song says, "He arose a victor from the dark domain, and He lives forever with His saints to reign!" In the book of Revelation, when John saw a vision of Christ's Kingdom, he wrote of those who had been washed in the Blood of the Lamb, "And they sing the song of Moses the servant of God, and the song of the Lamb, saying, Great and marvellous are thy works, Lord God Almighty; just and true are thy ways, thou King of saints" (Revelation 15:3).

It is good to sing the Song of the Lamb! He has already won the final battle on behalf of God's dear children.

CPSIA information can be obtained at www.ICGtesting.com
Printed in the USA
244153LV00005B/1/P